ASCENT
CENTER FOR TECHNICAL KNOWLEDGE

Autodesk® Revit® 2024
Collaboration Tools

Learning Guide
Metric Units - 1st Edition

ASCENT - Center for Technical Knowledge®
Autodesk® Revit® 2024
Collaboration Tools
Metric Units - 1st Edition

Prepared and produced by:

ASCENT Center for Technical Knowledge
630 Peter Jefferson Parkway, Suite 175
Charlottesville, VA 22911

866-527-2368
www.ASCENTed.com

Lead Contributor: Cherisse Biddulph

ASCENT - Center for Technical Knowledge (a division of Rand Worldwide Inc.) is a leading developer of professional learning materials and knowledge products for engineering software applications. ASCENT specializes in designing targeted content that facilitates application-based learning with hands-on software experience. For over 25 years, ASCENT has helped users become more productive through tailored custom learning solutions.

We welcome any comments you may have regarding this guide, or any of our products. To contact us please email: feedback@ASCENTed.com.

© ASCENT - Center for Technical Knowledge, 2023

The following are registered trademarks or trademarks of Autodesk, Inc., and/or its subsidiaries and/or affiliates in the USA and other countries: 123D, 3ds Max, ADSK, Alias, ATC, AutoCAD LT, AutoCAD, Autodesk, the Autodesk logo, Autodesk 123D, Autodesk Alias, Autodesk Docs, ArtCAM, Autodesk Forge, Autodesk Fusion, Autodesk Inventor, AutoSnap, BIM 360, Buzzsaw, CADmep, CAMduct, Civil 3D, Configurator 360, Dancing Baby (image), DWF, DWG, DWG (DWG logo), DWG Extreme, DWG TrueConvert, DWG TrueView, DWGX, DXF, Eagle, ESTmep, FBX, FeatureCAM, Flame, FormIt 360, Fusion 360, The Future of Making Things, Glue, Green Building Studio, InfraWorks, Instructables, Instructables (Instructables logo), Inventor, Inventor CAM, Inventor HSM, Inventor LT, Make Anything, Maya, Maya LT, Moldflow, MotionBuilder, Mudbox, Navisworks, Netfabb, Opticore, PartMaker, Pier 9, PowerInspect, PowerMill, PowerShape, Publisher 360, RasterDWG, RealDWG, ReCap, ReCap 360, Remake, Revit LT, Revit, Scaleform, Shotgun, Showcase, Showcase 360, SketchBook, Softimage, Tinkercad, TrustedDWG, VRED.

NASTRAN is a registered trademark of the National Aeronautics Space Administration.

All other brand names, product names, or trademarks belong to their respective holders.

General Disclaimer:

AS-REV2401-COL1MT-SG   //   IS-REV2401-COL1MT-SG

Contents

© 2023, ASCENT - Center for Technical Knowledge®

Chapter 4: Project Team Collaboration — 4-1

Preface

Autodesk® Revit® is a Building Information Modeling (BIM) tool, which can be used by more than one person working on a new project. This is an important feature in collaboration within a project, between projects, and with other users, firms, and disciplines.

The objective of the *Autodesk® Revit® 2024: Collaboration Tools* guide is to enable users who have a basic knowledge of Autodesk Revit to increase their productivity while working with other people on a team, either in the same firm or other firms as well as with other disciplines. It also covers linking Autodesk Revit files and linking or importing other CAD files. Practices are available for each of the primary disciplines covered by Autodesk Revit: architecture, MEP, and structure.

Topics Covered

- Set up project phasing

- Use groups

- Create and display a variety of design options

- Link Autodesk Revit files

- Use multi-discipline coordination, including Copy/Monitor and Coordination Review

- Import and export CAD and raster files, including exporting Revit models for energy analysis

- Understand, use, and set up worksharing in a server-based environment

Prerequisites

- Access to the 2024.1 version of the software, to ensure compatibility with this guide. Future software updates that are released by Autodesk may include changes that are not reflected in this guide. The practices and files included with this guide might not be compatible with prior versions (e.g., 2023).

- Users should be comfortable with the fundamentals of Autodesk Revit as taught in *Autodesk Revit: Fundamentals for Architecture, Autodesk Revit: Fundamentals for MEP*, or *Autodesk Revit: Fundamentals for Structure*. Knowledge of basic techniques is assumed, such as creating typical elements, copying and moving objects, creating and working with views, etc.

Note on Software Setup

This guide assumes a standard installation of the software using the default preferences during installation. Lectures and practices use the standard software templates and default options for the Content Libraries.

Note on Learning Guide Content

ASCENT's learning guides are intended to teach the technical aspects of using the software and do not focus on professional design principles and standards. The exercises aim to demonstrate the capabilities and flexibility of the software, rather than following specific design codes or standards, which can vary between regions.

Lead Contributor: Cherisse Biddulph

Cherisse is an Autodesk Certified Professional for Revit as well as an Autodesk Certified Instructor. She brings over 19 years of industry, teaching, and technical support experience to her role as a Learning Content Developer with ASCENT. With a passion for design and architecture, she has worked in the industry assisting firms with their Building Information Modeling (BIM) management and software implementation needs as they modernize to a BIM design environment. Although her main devotion is the Revit design product, she is also proficient in AutoCAD, Autodesk BIM 360, and Autodesk Navisworks. Today, Cherisse continues to expand her knowledge in the ever-evolving AEC industry and the software used to support it.

Cherisse Biddulph has been the Lead Contributor for *Autodesk Revit: Collaboration Tools* since 2020.

In This Guide

The following highlights the key features of this guide.

Feature	Description
Practice Files	The Practice Files page includes a link to the practice files and instructions on how to download and install them. The practice files are required to complete the practices in this guide.
Chapters	A chapter consists of the following: Learning Objectives, Instructional Content, Practices, Chapter Review Questions, and Command Summary.

- **Learning Objectives** define the skills you can acquire by learning the content provided in the chapter.
- **Instructional Content**, which begins right after Learning Objectives, refers to the descriptive and procedural information related to various topics. Each main topic introduces a product feature, discusses various aspects of that feature, and provides step-by-step procedures on how to use that feature. Where relevant, examples, figures, helpful hints, and notes are provided.
- **Practice** for a topic follows the instructional content. Practices enable you to use the software to perform a hands-on review of a topic. It is required that you download the practice files (using the link found on the Practice Files page) prior to starting the first practice.
- **Chapter Review Questions**, located close to the end of a chapter, enable you to test your knowledge of the key concepts discussed in the chapter.
- **Command Summary** concludes a chapter. It contains a list of the software commands that are used throughout the chapter and provides information on where the command can be found in the software.

Practice Files

To download the practice files for this guide, use the following steps:

1. Type the URL *exactly as shown below* into the address bar of your Internet browser to access the Course File Download page.

   Note: If you are using the ebook, you do not have to type the URL. Instead, you can access the page by clicking the URL below.

   ## https://www.ascented.com/getfile/id/polypterusPF

2. On the Course File Download page, click the **DOWNLOAD NOW** button, as shown below, to download the .ZIP file that contains the practice files.

3. Once the download is complete, unzip the file and extract its contents.

   The recommended practice files folder location is:
   C:\Revit Collaboration Tools Practice Files

   Note: It is recommended that you do not change the location of the practice files folder. Doing so may cause errors when completing the practices.

Stay Informed!

To receive information about upcoming events, promotional offers, and complimentary webcasts, visit:

www.ASCENTed.com/updates

Phasing, Groups, and Design Options

There are a variety of tools that can be used on complex projects:

- Phasing enables you to specify which project elements belong to a specific phase in the process of construction. You can create views that show each of these separate phases.

- Groups are sets of elements that can be inserted into a project. They can include both model and annotation elements. These groups can be saved to a separate file and then inserted or linked into multiple projects.

- Design options enable you to create different examples for part of a building, and then display each example in a separate view. Once you have decided which option to use, you can make the option part of the main model.

Learning Objectives

- Create and apply phases to elements.
- Create views to display different phases.
- Create groups of elements and annotations.
- Modify groups.
- Save groups as separate files.
- Create design options.
- Add existing and new elements to design options.
- Create views for design options.

1.1 Applying Project Phasing

Phases show distinct stages in a project's life. They are typically used with renovations and additions, as shown in Figure 1–1, or when a project involves several phases for its completion.

Figure 1–1

- There are two default phases included in the template files: **Existing** and **New Construction**. Many projects can be completed using just these two options, but additional phases can also be created for more complex projects.

All construction elements have two phase properties, *Phase Created* and *Phase Demolished*. This creates four potential status conditions for each element, regardless of how many phases are in a project:

- **Existing:** Created in an earlier phase and exists in the current phase.

- **New:** Created in the current phase.

- **Demolished:** Created in an earlier or existing phase and demolished in the current phase.

- **Temporary:** Created in the current phase and demolished in the current phase.

How To: Work with Phases

1. Open the view in which you want to work.

2. Without having any elements selected, in Properties, under the *Phasing* heading, select the *Phase* from the drop-down list, as shown in Figure 1–2. This becomes the current phase for this view.

   *Note: If you are working on a renovation project, start by modeling the building with the Phase set to **Existing**.*

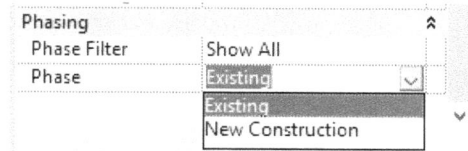

Properties of the view

Figure 1–2

3. Start modeling the elements. They take on the phase set in the current view.

- You can change the phase of elements by changing the *Phase Created* in the element's properties, as shown in Figure 1–3. Note that you can also demolish elements.

Properties of the element

Figure 1–3

Hint: Phases and Schedules

You can apply phases to schedules. When you create the schedule, include the *Phase Created* field and then use it in the *Filter* tab to limit the elements to a specific phase, as shown in Figure 1–4.

Figure 1–4

How To: Demolish Elements

1. In the *Modify* tab>Geometry panel, click 🔨 (Demolish).

2. Click on the elements that you want to demolish in the current phase, as shown in Figure 1−5.

Figure 1−5

- You can also select the elements you want to demolish and, in Properties, change the *Phase Demolished* value.

- Demolishing a wall also demolishes any doors or windows associated with that wall, as shown in Figure 1−6.

Figure 1−6

- To change an element so that it is no longer demolished, in Properties, set the *Phase Demolished* to **None**.

💡 Hint: Elements That Do Not Have Phases

Annotations (tags, text, or dimensions), view elements (elevations, sections, and callout views), and datum elements (grid lines and levels) do not have phases.

Curtain walls and beam systems include sub-elements that do not have phases. You need to select the primary curtain wall or beam system to change the phase.

When selecting multiple elements to apply a phase, click ▽:61 (Filter) in the Status Bar and clear the checkbox next to any annotations and curtain wall sub-elements (as shown in Figure 1–7) before modifying the phase in the properties.

Figure 1–7

- Non-phase elements can be hidden in views where you do not want them to show. For example, in Figure 1–8, hide (by element) grid lines 5-8 and then modify the length of grid lines A-C (change the 3D icon to 2D so the change only shows in the current view.) You could also change the crop region of the view.

Figure 1–8

Phases and Views

Duplicate a view for each phase you want to display. For example, you might want to show only the existing and demolished items in one view and the existing and new items, without the demolished items, in another view. You may also want to show the completed project without any of the previous phases, as shown in Figure 1–9.

Figure 1–9

Note: The look of the elements is determined by graphic overrides assigned to each phase filter.

The *Phase Filter*, specified in the view properties, determines which phases display in the view relative to the current phase:

- **None:** Displays all elements regardless of the current phase.

- **Show All:** Displays all phases up to the current phase, with all except the current phase, which is grayed out.

- **Show Complete:** Displays all construction up to the current phase.

- **Show Demo + New:** Displays the current phase and any demolished elements.

- **Show New:** Displays only elements created in the current phase.

- **Show Previous + Demo:** Displays elements created in previous phases and any demolished elements from the current phase.

- **Show Previous + New:** Displays elements created in the previous phase and any new elements created in the current phase.

- **Show Previous Phase:** Displays elements created in any previous phases.

Creating Phases

When you create new phases, you can specify the names and time sequence, set up phase filters, and specify graphic overrides for each phase.

How To: Create New Phases

1. In the *Manage* tab>Phasing panel, click ▦ (Phases).
2. In the Phasing dialog box, on the *Project Phases* tab, the existing phases display. Two phases, **Existing** and **New Construction** (as shown in Figure 1–10), come with most templates.

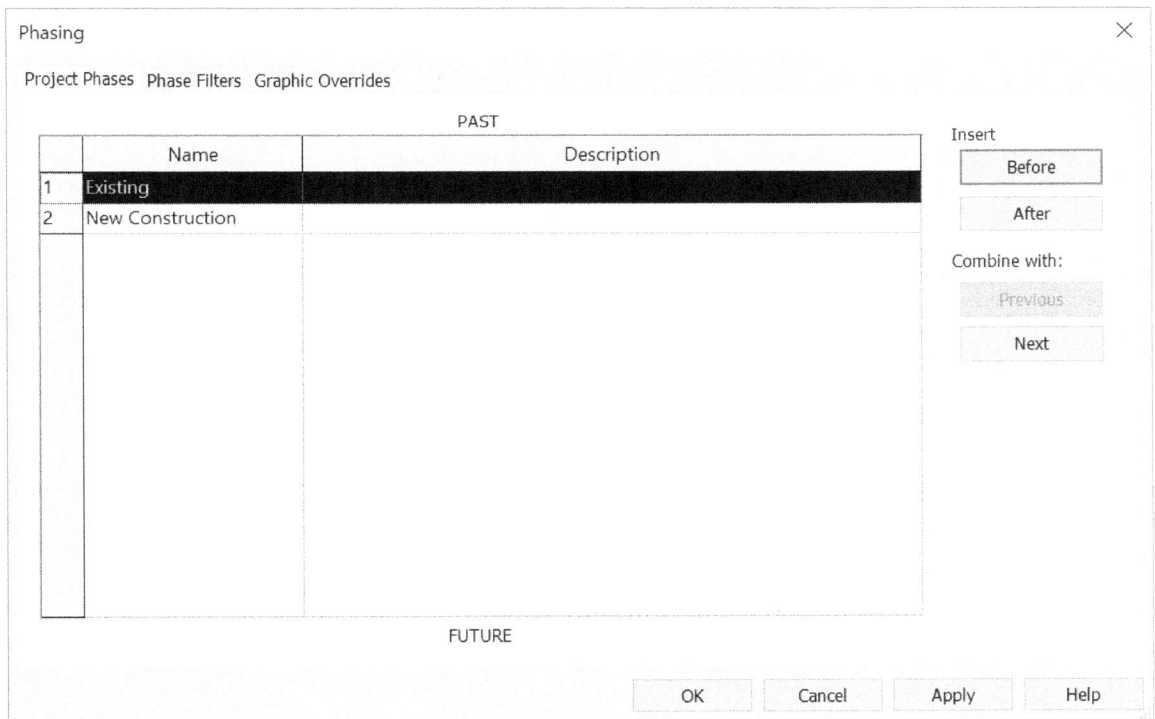

Figure 1–10

- The default phases can be renamed in this dialog box.

3. In the *Project Phases* tab, select a phase in the list. In the *Insert* area, click **Before** or **After**. You cannot change the order and need to be careful as you insert phases.

- New phases are numbered (Phase 1, Phase 2, etc.). Select the name to change it. You can also add a description for each phase.

- You can combine phases, as needed. Click **Previous** or **Next**. The elements on the combined phases take on the phase properties of the phase with which they were combined.

Note: You need to add the phase in the correct time sequence. Past and Future notations are at the top and bottom of the dialog box.

4. Select the *Phase Filters* tab, as shown in Figure 1–11. Several phase filters are supplied with the program and you can add more. Once you have a new phase filter, you define which of the phases display. If listed as **Overridden**, the graphic overrides display for the phase.

Phasing					✕

Project Phases   Phase Filters   Graphic Overrides

	Filter Name	New	Existing	Demolished	Temporary
1	Show All	By Category	Overridden	Overridden	Overridden
2	Show Complete	By Category	By Category	Not Displayed	Not Displayed
3	Show Demo + New	By Category	Not Displayed	Overridden	Overridden
4	Show New	By Category	Not Displayed	Not Displayed	Not Displayed
5	Show Previous + Demo	Not Displayed	Overridden	Overridden	Not Displayed
6	Show Previous + New	By Category	Overridden	Not Displayed	Not Displayed
7	Show Previous Phase	Not Displayed	Overridden	Not Displayed	Not Displayed

Figure 1–11

5. Select the *Graphic Overrides* tab, as shown in Figure 1–12. Set up the overrides, as required.

Phasing						✕

Project Phases   Phase Filters   Graphic Overrides

Phase Status	Projection/Surface		Cut		Halftone	Material
	Lines	Patterns	Lines	Patterns		
Existing	————		————Hidden		☐	Phase - Exist
Demolished	-------------		------------Hidden		☐	Phase - Demo
New	————		————	▓▓▓	☐	Phase - New
Temporary	·············		·············	///	☐	Phase - Temporary

Figure 1–12

6. Click **OK** to close the dialog box.

Practice 1a
Apply Project Phasing - Architectural

Practice Objectives

- Set custom phases in a project.
- Apply phases to elements.
- Apply phases to views.

In this practice, you will create several new phases and view the changes with the phase filters. You will also add some new elements in the existing building, as shown in Figure 1–13.

Phase 1   *Existing*   *Phase 2*

Figure 1–13

Task 1: Set up phases.

1. In the practice files *Architectural* folder, open **Arch-Phases-M.rvt**.

2. In the *Manage* tab>Phasing panel, click 🔲 (Phases).

3. In the Phasing dialog box, in the *Project Phases* tab, note that there are two phases: **Existing** and **New Construction**.

4. Click on **New Construction** and rename it to **Phase 1**. Enter **West Wing Addition** for the description, as shown in Figure 1–14.

5. In the *Insert* section, click **After** to add an additional phase after the last one. Keep the default name of **Phase 2** and enter **East Wing Addition** for the description, as shown in Figure 1–14.

Figure 1–14

6. Click **OK** to close the dialog box.

7. Select several individual elements from different parts of the building. (The number of elements you select does not matter.) In Properties, in the *Phasing* section, the *Phase Created* displays as **Phase 1**, as shown in Figure 1–15.

Figure 1–15

8. Select in an empty area in the view to clear the selection.

Task 2: Apply phases to views and elements.

1. Using the **Level 1** view, duplicate three new views and rename them **Level 1 - Existing**, **Level 1 - Phase 1**, and **Level 1 - Phase 2**.

2. Open the **Floor Plans: Level 1- Existing** view.

3. Select all elements in the middle building, as shown in Figure 1–16. Filter out any annotation elements, such as grid lines, tags, views, and elevations. If you have selected the windows in the halls outside of the middle building, hold down <Shift> and select them to remove them from the selection.

Figure 1–16

4. In Properties, change the *Phase Created* for these elements to **Existing**.

5. Click in the view to release the selection. The building elements should turn halftone when you clear the selection.

6. In Properties (with no elements selected), scroll down and set *Phase Filter* to **Show Complete** and *Phase* to **Existing**, as shown in Figure 1–17.

Phasing	☆
Phase Filter	Show Complete
Phase	Existing

Figure 1–17

7. Click in the view. Only the middle building displays but the grid lines on either side still display.

8. Turn on the crop region and verify that **Crop View** is on. Resize the crop region so only the middle building displays as shown in Figure 1–18.

Figure 1–18

9. Open the **Floor Plans: Level 1 - Phase 1** view.

10. Select the elements in the right (east) wing and the hall's walls and windows connecting to the middle building. Filter out any grids, views, and elevations, and change the *Phase Created* of these elements to **Phase 2**. In this case, the elements are removed from the view because the *Phase* of the view is set to **Phase 1**.

11. Turn on the crop region and verify that **Crop View** is on. Resize the crop region so the east wing grid lines do not display, as shown in Figure 1–19.

Figure 1–19

12. Without any elements selected, verify that the *Phase Filter* is set to **Show All** and the *Phase* is set to **Phase 1**.

13. In the *Modify* tab>Geometry panel, click 🔨 (Demolish). Select the four walls in the middle building that cross the long horizontal hallways, as shown in Figure 1–20.

Figure 1–20

14. Click ⬏ (Modify) and select one of the demolished walls. In Properties, scroll down to the *Phasing* area. Ensure that the *Phase Created* is set to **Existing** and *Phase Demolished* is set to **Phase 1**.

15. Open the **Floor Plans: Level 1 - Phase 2** view.

16. In Properties, without any elements selected, set the *Phase Filter* to **Show All** and change the *Phase* to **Phase 2**. The east wing is added and the demolished walls are removed, while the elements in the previous two phases are grayed out, as shown in Figure 1–21.

Figure 1–21

17. Modify the crop region so that it shows all of Phase 2 and part of the existing building. Hide the grid lines in the existing middle building by element, as shown in Figure 1−22.

Figure 1−22

18. In the existing building add several walls and doors with some of the doors along the existing walls, as shown in Figure 1−23.

Figure 1−23

19. Open the **Floor Plans: Level 1 - Phase 1** view to see that the walls added in Phase 2 do not display.

20. Save and close the project.

End of practice

Practice 1b
Apply Project Phasing - Structural

Practice Objectives

- Set custom phases in a project.
- Apply phases to elements.
- Apply phases to views.

In this practice, you will create phases and move the elements in the project to different phases. You will then view the changes with the phase filters, as shown in Figure 1–24.

Figure 1–24

Task 1: Set up phases.

1. In the practice files *Structural* folder, open **Struct-Phases-M.rvt**.

2. In the *Manage* tab>Phasing panel, click ⊞ (Phases).

3. In the Phasing dialog box, in the *Project Phases* tab, note that there is only the **New Construction** phase. You will divide the project into three phases.

4. Highlight **New Construction** with your cursor and rename the phase as **Phase 1**. Enter **Main Building** for the description.

5. In the *Insert* section, click **After** twice to add two additional phases after **Phase 1** and accept the default names of **Phase 2** and **Phase 3**. For the description, enter **Penthouse** for *Phase 2* and **Addition** for *Phase 3*, as shown in Figure 1–25.

Phasing			×

Project Phases Phase Filters Graphic Overrides

PAST

	Name	Description	Insert
1	Phase 1	Main Building	Before
2	Phase 2	Penthouse	After
3	Phase 3	Addition	Combine with:

Figure 1–25

6. Click **OK** to close the dialog box.

7. Select several individual elements from different parts of the building. (The number of elements you select does not matter.) In Properties, in the *Phasing* section, the *Phase Created* displays as **Phase 1**, as shown in Figure 1–26.

Properties	×

Multiple Categories Selected

Common (4)   Edit Type

Enable Analytical... ☑

Dimensions

Volume   <varies>

Identity Data

Image

Comments

Mark

Phasing

Phase Created   Phase 1

Phase Demolished None

Properties help   Apply

Figure 1–26

8. Select in an empty area in the view to clear the selection.

9. Save the project.

Task 2: Apply phases to elements.

1. Open the **Structural Plan: Penthouse** view. In Properties, verify that the *Phasing* area shows the *Phase* as **Phase 1**, as shown in Figure 1–27. This means that any new elements that are added will have their *Phase Created* as **Phase 1**.

Properties	✕
[icon] Structural Plan	▾

Structural Plan: Penthouse ⌄ ▦ Edit Type

Depth Clipping	No clip	⌃
Identity Data		⌂
View Template	<None>	
View Name	Penthouse	
Dependency	Independent	
Title on Sheet		
Referencing Sheet		
Referencing Detail		
Phasing		⌂
Phase Filter	Show All	
Phase	Phase 1	

Properties help   Apply

Figure 1–27

2. Select all of the Structural Beam Systems, Structural Columns, and Structural Framing (Girder). To do so, perform a crossing selection and filter out everything else.

3. In Properties, change the *Phase Created* to **Phase 2**. The Phase 2 elements are removed from the view because the view's *Phase* (in Properties) is set to Phase 1, but the elevator shaft and stair shaft walls remain (as shown in Figure 1–28) because their *Phase Created* is set to **Phase 1**.

Figure 1–28

In the following steps, you will add roofs using the **Structural Floor** command.

4. In the *Structure* tab>Structure panel, click (Floor: Structural). Do not use the Architectural Floor tool.

5. Add a roof slab to the top of the elevator shaft using the **Floor: 75mm Metal Roof Deck** type at a height of **2500mm** off the Roof level.

6. Repeat to add a roof to the stair shaft. The new slabs are added to Phase 1, represented by the red area in Figure 1–29.

   • To verify, select the new roofs. In Properties, look at the *Phasing* section and note that the *Phase Created* is **Phase 1**.

7. Click in an empty area in the view to clear the selection.

8. With no elements selected, the Properties display the properties for the active view. Change the *Phase* to **Phase 2**. The beams and columns now display.

9. In the View Control Bar, change the *Visual Style* to **Shaded** so the roofs are easier to see.

10. In the *Modify* tab>Geometry panel, click ⚒ (Demolish). Zoom in and select the metal roof decks. (Use <Tab> to select them.) Once they are demolished, they will turn red, as shown in Figure 1–29.

Figure 1–29

11. Click **Modify**.

12. Select one of the now demolished metal roof decks. In Properties, note that the element is listed as *Phase Created* in **Phase 1** and ***Phase Demolished*** in **Phase 2**, as shown in Figure 1–30. The dashed edges do not display in the view because they overlap the walls.

Phasing	⌃
Phase Created	Phase 1
Phase Demolished	Phase 2

Figure 1–30

13. Open the **Structural Plans: Level 1** view.

14. Select the structural columns, structural foundations, and walls connected to the arc area, as shown in Figure 1–31. In Properties, set the *Phase Created* to **Phase 3**. Use <Shift> to remove elements and use <Ctrl> to add elements.

Figure 1–31

15. Select grid line A.1. Right-click and select **Hide in View** by **Elements**.

16. Repeat the process of assigning the arc girders to Phase 3 in the **Structural Plans: Level 2**

17. Repeat in the **Structural Plans: Roof** view by first selecting the beam systems and changing them to Phase 3, and then selecting the rest of the structural framing and changing it to Phase 3.

18. Open the **3D Views: Front View**. It should display the existing building with the new roof slabs, as shown in Figure 1–32.

Figure 1–32

19. Save the project.

Task 3: Apply phases to views.

1. Use **Duplicate with Detailing** and create three new views of the **3D Views - Front View**. Rename them as **Front View - Phase 2**, **Front View - Phase 3**, and **Front View - Final**.

2. Rename Front View to **Front View - Phase 1**.

3. Open the **Front View - Phase 2** view.

4. In Properties, scroll down and change *Phase Filter* to **Show All** and *Phase* to **Phase 2**, as shown in Figure 1–33.

Phasing		⌃
Phase Filter	Show All	
Phase	Phase 2	

Figure 1–33

5. Click in the view. The existing building is grayed out and the new Penthouse phase displays with the demolished roof slabs in red, as shown in Figure 1–34.

Figure 1–34

6. Open the **Front View - Phase 3** view.

7. In Properties, set *Phase Filter* to **Show All** and the *Phase* to **Phase 3**. Now the existing building and the penthouse are grayed out and the new entrance structure displays as shown in Figure 1–35.

Figure 1–35

8. Open the **Front View - Final** view.

9. In Properties, set the *Phase Filter* to **Show Complete** and the *Phase* to **Phase 3**. All of the elements now display without any differences to the phases.

10. Save and close the project.

End of practice

Practice 1c
Apply Project Phasing - MEP

Practice Objectives

- Set custom phases in a project.
- Apply phases to elements.
- Apply phases to views.

In this practice, you will create phases and move the elements in the project to different phases. You will also draw new elements in different phases and view the changes with the phase filters, as shown in Figure 1–36.

Figure 1–36

Task 1: Set up phases.

1. In the practice files *MEP* folder, open **Mech-Phases-M.rvt**.

2. In the *Manage* tab>Phasing panel, click ▦ (Phases).

3. In the Phasing dialog box, in the *Project Phases* tab, note that there are two phases: **Existing** and **New Construction**. You will add two phases used for tenant build out.

4. Highlight **New Construction** with your cursor and rename the phase as **Tenant 1**.

5. In the *Insert* area, click **After** once and rename the new phase to **Tenant 2**, as shown in Figure 1–37.

Figure 1–37

6. Click **OK** to close the dialog box.

7. Select several individual elements from different parts of the building. (The number of elements you select does not matter.) In Properties, in the *Phasing* section, the *Phase Created* displays as **Tenant 1**, as shown in Figure 1–38.

Figure 1–38

8. Select in an empty area in the view to clear the selection.

9. Save the project.

Task 2: Apply phases to elements.

1. Working in the Mechanical>HVAC>Floor Plans: **1 - Mech** view, select all of the existing ductwork and air terminals and filter out anything else, as shown in Figure 1–39.

Figure 1–39

2. In Properties, change the *Phase Created* to **Existing** and note that the elements turn gray.

3. In Properties, with no element selected, note that the *Phase* is set to **Tenant 1**.

4. In the upper left area of the building, insert a VAV Unit, air terminals, and connecting ductwork, as shown in Figure 1–40.

    *Note: In this example, the VAV Unit's Elevation from Level is **3000mm** above Level 1 and the air terminals are **2500mm** above Level 1. The exact location and design are not critical.*

Figure 1–40

5. In Properties, with no elements selected, change the *Phase* to **Tenant 2** and draw an additional HVAC system. The Existing and Tenant 1 phases are grayed out and the current Phase displays in color, as shown in Figure 1−41.

Figure 1−41

Task 3: Apply phases to views.

1. Use **Duplicate with Detailing** and create three new views of **1- Mech** view. Rename them as **1 - Mech - Tenant 1**, **1 - Mech - Tenant 2**, and **1 - Mech - Final**.

2. Rename *1 - Mech* to **1 - Mech - Existing** and open it.

3. In Properties, change the *Phase* to **Existing**, as shown in Figure 1−42.

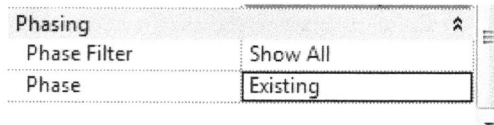

Figure 1−42

4. Open the **1 - Mech - Tenant 1** view and set the *Phase* to **Tenant 1**.

5. Open the **1 - Mech - Tenant 2** view and set the *Phase* to **Tenant 2**, if it is not already set.

6. Open the **1 - Mech - Final** view. Set the *Phase Filter* to **Show Complete** and the Phase to **Tenant 2**, as shown in Figure 1–43.

Figure 1–43

7. Save and close the project.

End of practice

1.2 Working with Groups

Groups are collections of one or more components in a specific configuration. Once a group is created, it will appear in the Project Browser in the Groups section. These groups can be placed in multiple locations with a single command, similarly to placing a family. If you edit a group, those changes will reflect in every instance of that group placed in the model. For example, if you are creating a hotel lobby, you can create a seating group (as shown in Figure 1–44) and then copy the group rather than placing the individual furniture components.

Model Groups : Model Group : Seating Area

Figure 1–44

Note: Groups are rarely used in MEP projects as systems do not work in groups.

There are three types of groups:

- **Model Groups:** Consists of model elements only.

- **Detail Groups:** Consists of detail or annotation elements only, including detail components, dimensions, tags, etc.

- **Model Groups with Attached Detail Groups:** Consists of a model group with the associated detail group attached to it.

- Model groups can be scheduled including the Count, Types, Reference Level and Origin Level Offset, as shown in Figure 1–45

<Model Groups Schedule>			
A	B	C	D
Count	Type	Reference Level	Origin Level Offset
4	Three Trees	Level 1	0
2	Three Trees	Level 2	100
4	Two Trees	Level 1	500
2	Two Trees	Level 2	300

Figure 1–45

Creating Groups

You can create groups by selecting elements and then using the **Group** command or by starting the command first and then adding the elements to the group. If you start the command first, anything you insert or draw during the process of creating the group is added to it.

How To: Create a Group Using Preselected Elements

1. Select the elements you want to include in the group.

2. In the *Modify | Multi-Select* tab>Create panel, click [icon] (Create Group) or type **GP**.

3. Enter a name in the Create Model Group dialog box, as shown in Figure 1−46. If you want to modify the group before creating it, select **Open in Group Editor**.

Create Model Group   ✕

Name: Office Cubicle|

☐ Open in Group Editor

OK   Cancel   Help

Figure 1−46

Note: If only Detail elements are selected, a similar dialog box opens. If you select both Model and Detail elements, you are prompted to name both the Model Group and the Attached Detail Group.

4. Click **OK** to create the group.

5. By default, the group origin is at the center of the group. Click and drag the origin to a new location, as shown in Figure 1−47. The new origin is used by any new instances of the group.

Figure 1−47

- Most elements can be grouped, including walls, components, and annotation, as long as the elements are compatible with each other.

- If you include a window, door, or other host-based element in a group, you need to place it on the type of host it is looking for.

How To: Create a Detail Group

1. Select the view-specific elements you want to include in the group, such as text, symbols, or detail components, as shown in Figure 1–48.

Figure 1–48

2. In the *Annotate* tab>Detail panel, expand ⬚ (Detail Group) and select ⬚ (Create Group).

3. In the Create Detail Group dialog box, enter a name for the detail group, as shown in Figure 1–49, and click **OK**.

Figure 1–49

- Alternatively, in the *Architecture* or *Structure* tab>Model panel, expand ⬚ (Model Group) and click ⬚ (Create Group). In the Create Group dialog box, name the group and select **Detail**, then select the elements.

How To: Create a Group and Add Elements

1. In the *Architecture* or *Structure* tab>Model panel, expand [⬚] (Model Group) and click [⬚] (Create Group).

2. In the Create Group dialog box, name the group and specify the type of group, either **Model** or **Detail**, as shown in Figure 1–50.

Create Group	✕
Name:	Office Cubicle
Group Type	
⦿ Model	
○ Detail	
OK Cancel Help	

Figure 1–50

3. Click **OK**.

4. The Group Editor opens with the Edit Group panel, as shown in Figure 1–51.

Add   Remove   Attach   Finish   Cancel

Edit Group

Figure 1–51

> *Note: Elements that are not part of the group are grayed out.*

5. Add elements to the group.

- Click [⬚] (Add) or type **AP** and select any existing elements you want to include in the group.

- Anything you draw or insert while in the Group Editor is added to the group.

  > *Note: The type of elements that you can select or insert depends on the Group Type* (**Model** *or* **Detail**).

- If you copy added elements, they will become a part of the group.

- Click ⌧ (Remove) or type **RG** to remove existing elements from the group. The elements are not removed from the project unless you delete them.

- To add or remove multiple elements from the group, hold <Ctrl> when selecting the elements.

- Click ⌂ (Attach) or type **AD** to add detail elements to a model group. The Create Model Group and Attached Detail Group dialog box displays, as shown in Figure 1-52. The *Model Group Name* is preset and you are required to add the *Attached Detail Group Name*.

  *Note: You cannot select detail elements with **Add** when editing a model group.*

Figure 1-52

Using Groups in a Project

You can add groups to a project by selecting them in the Project Browser, in the *Groups* node, and dragging them into the view, as shown in Figure 1-53. You can also use the **Place Group** commands.

Figure 1-53

- If a model group has a detail group, you need to attach it separately.

How To: Add Groups from the Ribbon

1. **For Model Groups:** In the *Architecture* or *Structure* tab> Model panel, expand ⌷ (Model Group) and click ⌷ (Place Model Group).

OR

   For Detail Groups: In the *Annotate* tab>Detail panel, expand ⌷ (Detail Group) and click ⌷ (Place Detail Group).

2. In Properties, in the Type Selector, select the group you want to add.

3. Click in the drawing screen to place the group. You can add multiple copies.

- If you selected a model group with a hosted element (such as a door or window) that does not include the host (wall), you can only place one group at a time.

- In some cases, when there are hosted and non-hosted elements in the same group, pick in the model to place the group and then move it so that the hosted element is on the correct host as shown in Figure 1–54. In the *Modify | Model Groups* tab>Edit Pasted panel, click ✓ (Finish).

Figure 1–54

How To: Attach Detail Groups to Model Groups

1. Select a model group that has a related detail group.

2. In the *Modify | Model Groups* tab>Group panel, click ⌷ (Attached Detail Groups).

3. In the Attached Detail Group Placement dialog box, select the detail groups that you to want attach to the model group, as shown in Figure 1–55.

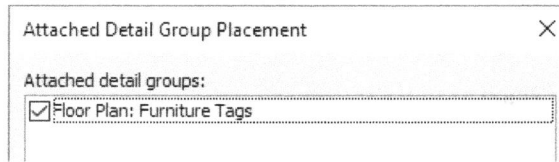

Attached Detail Group Placement	✕

Attached detail groups:
☑ Floor Plan: Furniture Tags

Figure 1–55

4. Click **OK**.

*   Remove detail groups from the model group by following the same process, but clearing the checkmark next to the group name in the dialog box.

Modifying Groups

Groups can be copied, moved, mirrored, and rotated like most elements in the program. You can also cut, copy, and paste them to the clipboard. Some properties can be changed for individual group instances, but most changes will need to be done in Group Edit mode. Group

Edit mode can be activated by selecting a group and clicking 🔲 (Edit Group) from the *Modify | Model Groups* tab>Group Panel or typing **EG**. Any changes made in Group Edit mode will be reflected in every instance of that group type.

*   If you no longer want an instance of a group to act as a group, as shown in Figure 1–56,

    select it and click 🔲 (Ungroup) in the Group panel, or type **UG**.

Grouped   *Ungrouped*

Figure 1–56

*   To delete a group definition from the project, you must first delete all instances of the group in the project. You can then select the group name in the Project Browser, right-click, and select **Delete**.

*   To modify individual instances of a group, use <Tab> to select one element in a group. Then, click on the *Group Member* icon (as shown in Figure 1–57), to remove the element from that instance of the group

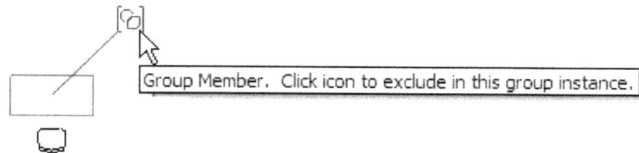

Group Member. Click icon to exclude in this group instance.

Figure 1–57

- To change a group to a different group, select one or more groups. In Properties, in the Type Selector, select another group's name, as shown in Figure 1–58.

  Note: If you are replacing groups, it helps to match the groups' origin and rotation.

Figure 1–58

- To make duplicates of groups, in the Project Browser, *Groups* node, right-click on the group and select **Duplicate**, or in Properties, click ⊞ (Edit Type) and **Duplicate...**. When you have copied the new group, make any changes as shown in Figure 1–59.

Group 1   *Copy of Group 1*

Figure 1–59

- To modify all instances of a group definition, in the *Modify | Model Groups* tab>Group panel, click (Edit Group) or type **EG**. In the Group Editor, make changes to the group as required. Use the floating Edit Group toolbar to add, remove, and attach elements.

- To change the name of a group, right-click on the group in the Project Browser and select **Rename**.

Groups in Other Projects

You can save groups to a project file to use in other projects. Groups can also be converted to links. This creates an additional project file but also changes the group in your project to link to the new project file.

How To: Save a Group as a File

1. In the *File* tab, expand 🖫 (Save As), expand 📖 (Library), and click 🗃 (Group).

2. In the Save Group dialog box, in the Group To Save drop-down list, select a group, as shown in Figure 1–60.

   *Note: Alternatively, right-click on the group name in the Project Browser and select **Save Group**.*

File name:	Same as group name
Files of type:	Revit Project (*.rvt)
Group To Save:	Model Group: Group 1 ⌄
	☑ Include attached detail groups as views

   Figure 1–60

3. Navigate to the folder in which you want to store the group.

4. Click **Save**.

How To: Use a File as a Group in a Project

1. Open the file in which you want to load the group.

2. In the *Insert* tab>Load from Library panel, click 🗃 (Load As Group).

3. In the Load File as Group dialog box, navigate to the folder in which the file is stored and select the file.

4. Click **Open**. The file is added as a group definition in the current project.

5. Insert the group in the project using one of the methods for placing a group.

- Any Revit project or family file can be loaded as a group.

- Because a group can be saved as a standard RVT project file, the groups can be edited externally from any project.

- When you reload the group into a project, an alert box opens if you are loading a file with the same name as an existing group in your project, as shown in Figure 1–61.

Figure 1–61

- Click **Yes** to replace all instances of the group with the new information.
- Click **No** to bring in the group with a new name incremented from the previous name.
- Click **Cancel** to stop the process.

How To: Use an Open File as a Group in Another Open File

1. Open a project file in which you want to place a group.
2. Open the file that you want to use as a group.
3. In the *Architecture* or *Structure* tab> Model panel, expand [icon] (Model Group) and click [icon] (Load as Group into Open Projects).
4. In the Load into Projects dialog box, select the projects into which you want the currently active project to be loaded as a group.
5. Click **OK**. The group is now available for use in the other projects.

How To: Convert a Group to a Link

1. Select the group that you want to convert to a link.
2. In the *Modify | Model Groups* tab>Group panel, click [icon] (Link).

3. In the Convert to Link dialog box (shown in Figure 1–62), select the method that you want to use.

Convert to Link   ✕

How do you want to convert the group?

→ Replace with a new project file
    Saves the group as a new project, and then removes the group instance and replaces it with
    a link to the new project.

→ Replace with an existing project file
    Removes the group instance and replaces it with a link to a project that already exists.

                                                              [Cancel]

Click here to learn more about converting groups

Figure 1–62

4. If you create a new project file, the Save Group dialog box opens. Specify the name and location of the file and click **Save**. The group becomes a linked model in the host project.

5. If you replace it with an existing project file, the Open dialog box opens. Locate the file you want to use to replace the existing group, and click **Open**. The new project file becomes a linked model in the host project.

Practice 1d
Work with Groups - Architectural

Practice Objectives

- Create a group.
- Place instances of a group in a project.
- Edit a group definition.
- Modify an instance of a group.

In this practice, you will group components, copy the group, modify the group, and modify one instance, as shown in Figure 1–63. You will also save the group to be used in another project.

Figure 1–63

Task 1: Create a group.

1. In the practice files *Architectural* folder, open **Arch-Groups-M.rvt**.
2. Add the component **M_Desk: 1525 x 762mm** against the left back wall.

    Note: Click ≣ (Thin Lines) in the Quick Access Toolbar or View tab>Graphics panel to help you see the exact placement of the panel.

3. Place a **M_Chair-Executive** in front of the desk and a **M_Cube Panel: 1525 x 1680** to the right of it, as shown in Figure 1–64. These components are already loaded into the project.

4. Place a **M_Fixed 0610 x 1830** window with a tag in the wall directly in front of the desk, as shown in Figure 1–64.

Figure 1–64

5. Select the three components, the window, and the tag.

6. In the *Modify | Multi-Select* tab>Create panel, click (Create Group).

7. Name the Model Group as **Test Station**, and the Attached Detail Group as **Tags**, as shown in Figure 1–65. Click **OK**.

Figure 1–65

8. Click on the Modify Group Origin control, as shown on the left in Figure 1–66, and drag it to the upper left corner of the desk, as shown on the right in Figure 1–66.

Figure 1–66

9. Click in an empty area in the view to clear the selection.

Task 2: Place instances of the group.

1. In the *Architecture* tab>Model panel, expand 🔲 (Model Group) and click 🔲 (Place Model Group).

2. In the Type Selector, verify that the name of the current group is **Test Station**.

   Note: Because this is a model group that includes hosted elements (the window) without the host element (the wall), you can only place one group at a time.

3. Place a copy of the group directly to the right of the original group using the Endpoint snap, as shown in Figure 1–67. Everything but the tag should be inserted.

Figure 1–67

4. Click ✔ (Finish) to complete the process.

5. Select the new group.

6. In the *Modify | Model Groups* tab>Group panel, click 🖳 (Attached Detail Groups).

7. In the Attached Detail Group Placement dialog box, select the **Floor Plan: Tags** detail group and click **OK**. The tag is added to the instance of the group.

Task 3: Edit the group definition.

1. The current group is still selected. In the *Modify | Model Groups* tab>Group panel, click 🔲 (Edit Group).

2. In the Group Editor, in the floating Edit Group panel, click 🔲 (Remove).

3. Select the window to remove it from the group.

4. Click ✔ (Finish).

5. The windows are no longer involved in the groups but they are still in the drawing. A warning dialog box opens, indicating that the attached detail group is removed, as shown in Figure 1−68. Click **OK**.

Figure 1−68

6. Place two more copies of the model group **Test Station** in the project. The new groups do not include the window.

Task 4: Modify an instance of a group.

1. The last group does not need the last cubicle wall. Hover over the element that you want to exclude, press <Tab> until it highlights, and select the element, as shown in Figure 1–69.

Group Member icon

Figure 1–69

2. Click the Group Member icon to only exclude the wall from that group. Click in an empty space in the view to complete the process. The cubicle wall is only excluded from that group.

Task 5: Save the group as a file.

1. In the Project Browser, expand the *Groups*>**Model** node, right-click on the **Test Station** group name, and select **Save Group**.

2. In the Save Group dialog box, navigate to your practice files folder and save the group with the same name as the group. The group is now a .RVT and can be loaded as a group into other projects.

3. Save and close the project.

End of practice

Practice 1e
Work with Groups - Structural

Practice Objectives

- Create a group of model and annotation elements.
- Add copies of the group to a project.
- Modify the elements of one group.

In this practice, you will place bracing in a framing elevation and then group the bracing and its associated tags as shown in Figure 1–70. You will also add the group to another bay and copy it to further bays. You will ungroup and modify one group and use the elements to create another group.

Figure 1–70

Task 1: Add bracing.

1. In the practice files *Structural* folder, open **Struct-Groups-M.rvt**.
2. Open the **Elevations (Framing Elevation): West Bracing** view.
3. Zoom in to display the **00 GROUND FLOOR** and **TOS-1ST FLOOR** level heads.

4. In the *Structure* tab>Structure panel, click ⊠ (Brace).

5. In the *Modify | Place Brace* tab>Tag panel, click (Tag on Placement) to toggle it on.
6. In the Type Selector, select **M_HSS Hollow Structural Section: HSS152.4x152.4x9.5**.

7. Draw from the midpoint of the beam located on the 1st Floor to the centerline of the column at the base, as shown in Figure 1–71. Do the same on both sides.

Figure 1–71

8. Press <Esc> or click **Modify** to end the command.

Task 2: Create and place groups.

1. Select the braces and the tags.

2. In the *Modify | Multi Select* tab>Create panel, click ⬚ (Create Group).

3. Name the groups **Brace Frame A-Model** and **Brace Frame A-Tags**, as shown in Figure 1–72.

Figure 1–72

4. Click **OK**.

5. Move the Group Origin to the lower left corner, as shown in Figure 1–73, to change the insertion point of the group. Make sure to snap to the intersection of the column and beam.

Figure 1–73

6. Select in an empty area in the view to clear the selection.

7. Place an instance of the new group. In the *Structure* tab>Model panel, expand ⌷ (Model Group) and click ⌷ (Place Model Group).

8. In the Type Selector, verify that the name of the current group is **Brace Frame A - Model**.

   Note: The group moves into the correct location once you complete the process.

9. In the *Modify | Model Groups* tab>Edit Pasted panel, click ✓ (Finish).

10. Select the group. In the *Modify | Model Groups* tab>Group panel, click ⌷ (Attached Detail Groups).

11. In the Attached Detail Group Placement dialog box, select **Elevation: Brace Bay A-Tags**.

12. Click **OK**. The bracing is labeled.

13. Copy the group with details up to the 13th floor. Select both the brace group and the attached detail group.

14. In the *Modify | Multi-Select* tab>Modify panel, click ⌷ (Copy).

15. In the Options Bar, select **Multiple** and **Constrain** (this forces the copy to only move horizontally or vertically).

16. Copy the groups to every level up to the 13th floor.

17. Zoom in on the 13th floor bay, as shown in Figure 1–74. This bay requires a modification because of the difference in elevation.

Figure 1–74

18. Select the bracing, and in the *Modify | Model Groups* tab> Group panel, click ⬚ (Ungroup).

19. Modify the braces so that they extend up to the framing, as shown in Figure 1–75.

Figure 1–75

20. Select the revised braces and tags. Create a new group with an attached detail group named **Brace Frame B-Model** and **Brace Frame B-Tags**.

21. Save and close the project.

End of practice

1.3 Using Design Options

Design options are isolated collections of model elements used to provide a variety of potential configurations for a certain area within a building model. For example, you could design several roof options, window layouts, or entry areas and view each in context with the main building.

Design option sets are used to gather and manage design options for a certain area. Areas of the building model that do not have design options are called the main model. Each design option set will have a primary option that will show by default when viewing the main model. For example, you can create a design option set with options for an A-frame roof (as shown in Figure 1–76) and a curved roof (as shown in Figure 1–77).

Figure 1–76   Figure 1–77

- Design option sets and design options are automatically organized alphanumerically by name. Make sure to use a clear and descriptive naming convention to help you efficiently manage your design option sets.

- If the design option affects multiple disciplines and requires design options in more than one model, such as a roof that requires both architectural and structural options, coordinating these naming conventions across the models can help prevent confusion when incorporating the final decisions.

    Note: Design options are rarely used in MEP projects as systems do not work in the options.

The design options tools are located in the *Manage* tab>Design Options panel, as shown in Figure 1–78, with additional tools in the Status Bar, as shown in Figure 1–79.

Figure 1–78

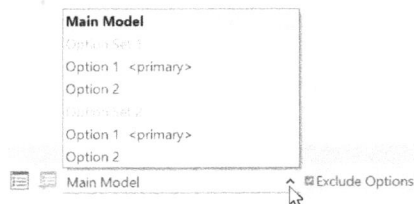

Figure 1–79

- When you have decided which design option will be the final configuration, you will set that option to be **primary** and accept the primary design option for that design option set. When you accept the primary design option, all other design options within that design option set will be permanently deleted and all model elements within them removed from the model.

- If other members of your team are linking your model into theirs, only the primary design option will be visible to them. Non-primary design options will not be available for interdisciplinary coordination.

How To: Set Up Design Options

1. In the *Manage* tab>Design Options panel, or in the Status Bar, click ⊟ (Design Options). The Design Options dialog box opens, as shown in Figure 1–80.

   Note: You can have as many option sets and options under a set, as needed. Each set always contains one primary option.

Design Options	✕
Now Editing:	Edit
Main Model	Edit Selected
	Finish Editing
	Option Set
	New
	Rename
	Accept Primary...
	Delete...
	Option
	New
	Make Primary
	Rename
	Duplicate
	Delete
	Close Help

Figure 1–80

2. In the *Option Set* area, click **New**. An option set with a corresponding option is created, as shown in Figure 1–81.

Figure 1–81

3. To add more options, select the Option Set title. In the *Option* area in the dialog box, rename the options so that they convey more information. In the *Option Set* or *Option* area, click **Rename** and type a new name in the Rename dialog box. As you create more design options and sets, they will be automatically sorted in alphanumeric order.

4. Once you have defined the option sets and options, you are ready to work on the various options. Close the dialog box.

• When you have added design options, you can set the current design option in the *Manage* tab or in the Status Bar, as shown in Figure 1–82.

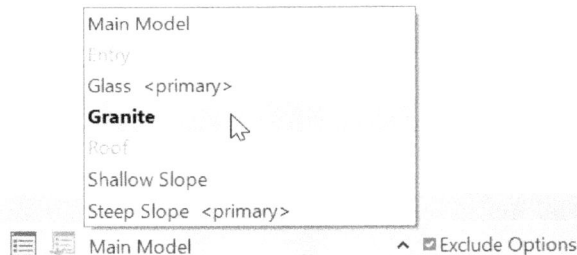

Figure 1–82

How To: Add Existing Elements to Design Options

1. In the Status Bar or *Manage* tab>Design Options panel, verify that **Main Model** displays as the active design option, as shown in Figure 1–83.

Figure 1–83

2. In the Status Bar, next to the active design option, clear the **Active Only** option. This enables you to select elements that are not in the current design option.

3. Select the elements that you want to include in a design option. The *Modify* tab displays.

4. Switch to the *Manage* tab. In the Design Options panel, click ⊞ (Add to Set).

5. In the Add to Design Option Set dialog box, expand the drop-down list and select the design option set, then select the option(s) to which you want to add the selected elements, as shown in Figure 1−84. You can select more than one option.

Figure 1−84

6. Click **OK** to close the dialog box. The elements are added to the option and can no longer be modified in the main model.

• Only elements in the primary design option display in standard views. They cannot be selected unless you clear **Exclude Options** in the Status Bar before selecting.

• **Exclude Options** is only available in the Status Bar if design options have been set up in the project.

How To: Add New Elements to a Design Option

1. Set a design option to be current in the active design option drop-down list in the Status Bar or in the *Manage* tab>Design Options panel, as shown in Figure 1−85.

Figure 1−85

2. Only the elements that are part of the active design option display in black. Elements in the main model are grayed out, as shown in Figure 1–86.

Figure 1–86

3. Use standard commands to add or modify elements in the design option. For example, you can move the seating and add other chairs and tables on the floor plan.

4. Set the active design option to **Main Model** when you are finished.

Viewing Design Options

You can set up views and view templates that specify design options. These can then be used to quickly see the various design options without having to edit them, as shown in Figure 1–87.

Design Option 1   Design Option 2

Figure 1–87

How To: View Design Options

1. Create a view (a 3D view, plan, elevation, or section) that displays the information that you want to present.

2. In the view, open the Visibility/Graphic Overrides dialog box (type **VV** or **VG**)

    • Alternatively, you can set the current view's design option from the *Graphics* area in Properties.

3. In the Visibility/Graphic Overrides dialog box, in the *Design Options* tab, select a design option from the drop-down list for each design option set, as shown in Figure 1–88. **<Automatic>** displays the primary option or the option that is currently being edited. Setting the view to a specific choice displays that option regardless of what is being edited.

Figure 1–88

• If elements in a design option display in a view, you can click 🗔 (Pick to Edit) in the Design Options panel and select one of the elements to activate that option.

How To: Incorporate Design Options into the Main Model

Once you have decided which design option will become part of the final model, you will incorporate it into the main model and remove all of the secondary design options within that set.

1. Set the active design option to **Main Model**.

    *Note: If you did not set the active option to Main Model, you must select **Finish Editing** in the dialog box to continue the process.*

2. In the *Manage* tab, select ▤ (Design Options) from the Design Options panel.

3. Select the option you want to keep and click **Make Primary** from the *Options* area of the dialog box.

4. Select the option set and click **Accept Primary...** from the *Options Set* area of the dialog box.

5. An alert box opens as shown in Figure 1–89, warning you that all secondary options are going to be deleted. Click **Yes** if you are sure.

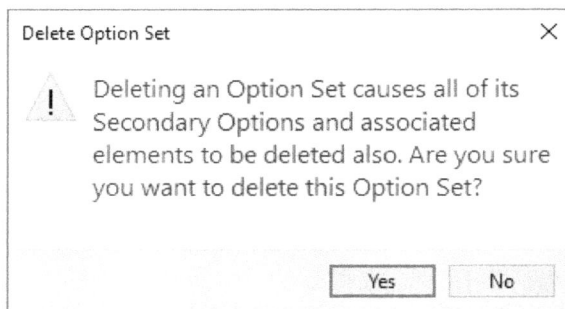

Figure 1–89

6. If views are associated with the option, you are prompted to delete the associated views, as shown in Figure 1–90. Select the view(s) and click **Delete**.

Figure 1–90

7. Close the Design Options dialog box.

Practice 1f
Use Design Options - Architectural

Practice Objectives

- Set up design options.
- Draw elements in each design option.
- Create views that show variations on the design options.

In this practice, you will create two design option sets and several options for each set. You will modify the elements in each design option and create views that display the options, such as the one shown in Figure 1–91.

Figure 1–91

- As design options are rarely used with the Revit system tools, MEP engineers can work through this practice to understand the process.

Task 1: Set up design options.

1. In the practice files *Architectural* folder, open **Arch-DesignOps-M.rvt**.

2. In the *Manage* tab>Design Options panel or in the Status Bar, click ⊟ (Design Options).

3. In the Design Options dialog box, in the *Option Set* area, click **New**. A new option set and a primary option are created, as shown in Figure 1–92.

Figure 1–92

4. Select **Option Set 1** and in the *Option Set* area, click **Rename**.

5. In the Rename dialog box, type **Main Roof** for the new name and click **OK**.

6. Select **Option 1 <primary>** and in the *Option* area, click **Rename**. Type **Shallow Slope** for the new name and click **OK**.

7. In the *Option* area, click **New** twice to add two more options and rename them as **Medium Slope** and **Steep Slope**.

8. Create an additional option set called **Entry Roof** and three options: **Curved** (as the <primary>), **Angled**, and **Stepped**, as shown in Figure 1–93.

Figure 1–93

9. In the **Main Roof** option set, select **Medium Slope** and click **Make Primary**.

10. Close the Design Options dialog box.

Task 2: Create main roof design options.

1. In the *Manage* tab>Design Options panel (as shown on the left in Figure 1–94) or in the Status Bar (as shown on the right in Figure 1–94), activate the **Main Roof>Medium Slope <primary>** option using the active design option drop-down list. The main model is grayed out.

Figure 1–94

2. Open the **Floor Plans: Roof** view.

3. Draw a **Roof by Footprint** with a deep overhang, all edges sloped, and a medium slope angle, as shown in Figure 1–95.

Figure 1–95

4. In the *Modify | Create Roof Footprint* tab>Mode panel, click ✔ (Finish Edit Mode).

5. When prompted to attach highlighted walls to the roof, select **Don't Attach**.

6. View the roof in a 3D view.

7. Return to the **Floor Plans: Roof** view. Set the active design option to **Main Roof>Steep Slope**. The main model is grayed out and the medium sloped roof is toggled off.

8. Draw a **Roof by Footprint** using a steep slope angle. When finished, click **Finish Edit Mode** and select **Don't attach**.

9. Repeat the process using the **Shallow Slope** design option and a shallow roof slope. When finished, click **Finish Edit Mode** and select **Don't attach**.

10. Set the active design option to **Main Model**. The primary **Medium Slope** design option displays.

11. Duplicate the default 3D view three times and rename them as **3D Steep Roof**, **3D Medium Roof**, and **3D Shallow Roof**.

12. Within the **3D Shallow Roof** view, open the Visibility/Graphic Overrides dialog box and click on the *Design Options* tab. In the *Design Option* column, set the design option for the *Main Roof* to **Shallow Slope**, as shown in Figure 1–96.

Figure 1–96

13. Repeat Step 12 for the **3D Steep Roof** and **3D Medium Roof** views.

14. Save the project.

Task 3: Create entry roof design options.

1. Return to the **Floor Plans: Roof** view.

2. Set the active design option to **Entry Roof>Curved**. The main model and main roof are grayed out.

3. Open the **Floor Plans: Level 2** view.

4. Use **Roof by Footprint** to draw a curved flat roof over the entry area, as shown in Figure 1−97. You can use the **Spline** or **Arc** sketch options. Uncheck **Defines Slope** and use a generic roof type.

Figure 1−97

5. In the *Modify | Create Roof Footprint* tab>Mode panel, click ✔ (Finish Edit Mode).

6. Create additional flat roofs similar to those shown in Figure 1−98 for the **Angled** and **Stepped** entry roof options.

Figure 1−98

7. Return the active design option to the **Main Model**. The curved roof displays as it is the primary design option that shows at this level.

8. Save the project.

Task 4: Create views of design options.

1. Switch to the **3D Medium Roof** view that displays both the main and entry roofs. Orbit the view so that you can see both roofs.

2. Select a level and type **VH** to hide them in this view.

3. Type **VV** to open the Visibility/Graphic Overrides dialog box.

4. In the *Design Options* tab, specify the *Design Options* for the sets as follows and click **OK**.

    *   *Entry Roof:* **Curved <primary>**

    *   *Main Roof:* **Medium Slope <primary>**

5. The 3D view should show the curved and medium sloped roofs, as shown in Figure 1−99.

Figure 1−99

6. Open the **3D Shallow Roof** view and hide the levels.

7. Open the Visibility/Graphic Overrides dialog box and in the *Design Options* tab, specify the *Design Options* for the sets as follows and click **OK**.

    *   *Entry Roof:* **Stepped**

    *   *Main Roof:* **Shallow Slope**

The new layout displays as shown in Figure 1–100.

Figure 1–100

8. Repeat this for the **3D Steep Roof** view, Select a level and type **VH** to hide them in this view.

9. Open the Visibility/Graphic Overrides dialog box and in the *Design Options* tab, specify the *Design Options* for the sets as follows and click **OK**.

    *   *Entry Roof:* **Angled**
    *   *Main Roof:* **Steep Slope**

    The new layout displays as shown in Figure 1–101.

Figure 1–101

10. Switch between the various views to see the differences.

11. Save and close the project.

End of practice

Practice 1g
Use Design Options - Structural

Practice Objectives

- Set up design options.
- Draw elements in each design option.
- Create views that show variations on the design options.

In this practice, you will create two design options. You will modify the elements in each design option and create views that display the options, such as the one shown in Figure 1–102.

Figure 1–102

Task 1: Set up design options.

1. In the practice files *Structural* folder, open **Struct-DesignOps-M.rvt**.

2. In the *Manage* tab>Design Options panel or in the Status Bar, click ▤ (Design Options).

3. In the Design Options dialog box, in the *Option Set* area, click **New**. A new option set and a primary option are created, as shown in Figure 1–103.

Figure 1–103

4. Select **Option Set 1** and in the *Option Set* area, click **Rename**.

5. In the Rename dialog box, set the new name as **Penthouse Roof** and click **OK**.

6. Select **Option 1 <primary>** and in the *Option* area, click **Rename**. Set the name as **Flat Roof** and click **OK**.

7. In the *Option* area, click **New** twice to add two more options and rename them as **A-Frame** and **Arched Roof**, as shown in Figure 1–104.

Figure 1–104

8. Close the Design Options dialog box.

9. Save the project.

Task 2: Add structural elements to design options.

1. In the *Manage* tab>Design Options panel (as shown on the left in Figure 1–105) or in the Status Bar (as shown on the right in Figure 1–105), select the **Flat Roof <primary>** option in the active design option drop-down list. The model is grayed out.

Figure 1–105

2. Open the **Structural Plans: Penthouse** view.

3. In the Status Bar, next to the active design options, clear the **Active Only** option. This enables you to select elements that are not in the current design option.

4. Using a window selection, select all of the objects in the view.

5. In the *Modify | Multi-Select* tab>Selection panel, click ▽ (Filter).

6. In the Filter dialog box, select **Structural Beam Systems**, **Structural Columns**, **Structural Framing (Girder)**, and **Structural Framing (Joist)**, as shown in Figure 1–106, and click **OK**.

Figure 1–106

7. In the *Manage* tab>Design Options panel or in the Status Bar, click ⬚ (Add to Set).

8. Read and close the warning dialog box.

9. Switch to the **3D Views: Front N/E** view. The **Flat Roof <primary>** design option's elements display while all the other elements are grayed out, as shown in Figure 1–107.

Figure 1–107

10. Duplicate the **Front N/E** view three times and rename one of the duplicated views **Front N/E - Flat Roof**.

11. In the **Front N/E - Flat Roof** view, type **VV** to open the Visibility/Graphic Overrides dialog box.

12. In the *Design Options* tab, set the *Design Option* for the *Penthouse Roof* to **Flat Roof <primary>**, as shown in Figure 1–108.

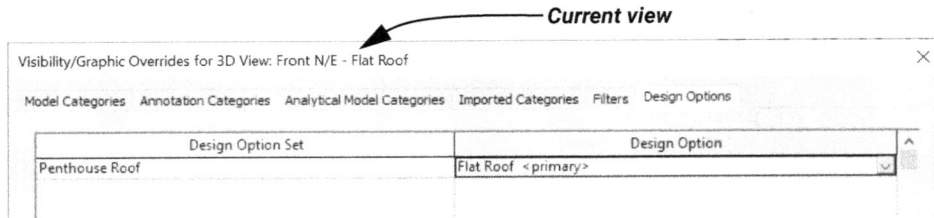

Figure 1–108

13. Click **OK**.

14. Rename the other duplicated views as **Front N/E - A-Frame Roof** and **Front N/E - Arched Roof**.

15. In each of the views, open the Visibility/Graphic Overrides dialog box and change the *Design Option* to the corresponding design option for that view.

16. Click **OK**.

17. Open the **Front N/E - A-Frame Roof** view and set the active design option in the Status Bar to **A-Frame**.

18. Delete the three flat beam systems in the view, as shown in Figure 1–109.

Figure 1–109

19. Open the south elevation view and start the **Beam** command.

20. In the Options Bar, set the *Placement Plane* to **Grid: D**, as shown in Figure 1–110. Verify **Chain** is unchecked.

Figure 1–110

21. Draw an A-frame roof using the **M_W-Wide Flange W250X17.9** beam, as shown in Figure 1–111. Use **Reference Planes** as needed.

Figure 1–111

22. Open the **Penthouse** view and array the A-frame beams. In the Options Bar, set the following, as shown in Figure 1–112:

- Uncheck **Group and Associate**
- *Number:* **20**
- *Move To:* **Last**

Figure 1–112

23. Open the **Front N/E A-Frame Roof** view to review the roof, as shown in Figure 1–113.

Figure 1–113

24. Switch to the **Front N/E - Arched Roof** view and set the active design option in the Status Bar to **Arched Roof**.

25. Delete the three beam systems in the view.

26. Open the south elevation view. In the Options Bar, set the *Placement Plane* to **Grid: D**. **Chain** should be unchecked.

27. Draw an arched roof using the **M_W-Wide Flange W250X17.9** beam, as shown in Figure 1–114. Use **Reference Planes** as needed.

Figure 1–114

28. Open the **Penthouse** view and array the arched beams. Set the Options Bar settings to the following:

- Uncheck **Group and Associate**
- *Number:* **20**
- *Move To:* **Last**

29. Open the **Front N/E - Arched Roof** view to review the roof, as shown in Figure 1–115.

Figure 1–115

30. Open the **Front N/E** view. In the Status Bar, set the active design option to **Main Model**. This ends the design options editing, and the flat roof displays as it is the primary design option that shows at this level.

31. Switch between the various **Front N/E** views to see the differences.

32. Save and close the project.

End of practice

Chapter Review Questions

1. When you want to demolish some elements, as shown in Figure 1–116, in what phase should the elements be?

Figure 1–116

  a. New Construction

  b. Existing

  c. Demolition

2. When creating a view that displays the *Phase* **New Construction** along with the existing and demolished elements, as shown in Figure 1–117, which of the Phase Filters do you use?

Figure 1–117

  a. Show All

  b. Show Complete

  c. Show Previous + New

  d. Show Previous Phase

3. Which statement is true regarding *Option Set* and *Option*, as shown in Figure 1–118?

Option Set

| New |
| Rename |
| Accept Primary... |
| Delete... |

Option

| New |
| Make Primary |
| Rename |

Figure 1–118

a. You can have multiple options but only one option set.

b. You can have multiple options without any option set.

c. You can have multiple option sets without any options.

d. You can have multiple option sets with multiple options in each set.

4. What method do you use to set up a view to display specific design options?

a. Set the active design option.

b. Select the primary design option in the Design Options dialog box.

c. Open the Visibility/Graphic Overrides dialog box and select the option from the *Design Options* tab.

d. Right-click in the view and select **Override Graphics in view>By Element**.

5. Which are the type of groups that can be created in Revit? (Select all that apply.)

a. Annotative

b. Component

c. Detail

d. Model

6. While in the Group Editor, how do you add tags to an existing group, as shown in Figure 1–119, so that it creates a related detail group?

Figure 1–119

a. Drag and drop the tags group from the Project Browser on to the group.

b. In the Edit Group panel, click (Add) and select existing tags.

c. In the Edit Group panel, click (Attach) and specify the tags group.

d. Add the tags using (Tag by Category).

7. You can use the contents of an entire open project as a group in another project.

a. True

b. False

Command Summary

Button	Command	Location
Phases		
	Demolish	• **Ribbon**: *Modify* tab>Geometry panel
	Phases	• **Ribbon**: *Manage* tab>Phasing panel
Design Options		
Main Model ▾ (drop-down list)	**Active Design Option**	• **Ribbon:** *Manage* tab>Design Options panel • **Status Bar**
	Add to Set	• **Ribbon:** *Manage* tab>Design Options panel • **Status Bar**
	Design Options	• **Ribbon:** *Manage* tab>Design Options panel • **Status Bar**
	Pick to Edit	• **Ribbon:** *Manage* tab>Design Options panel
Groups		
	Add to Group	• **Floating Panel:** Edit Group • **Shortcut**: AP (when a group is in edit mode)
	Attach Detail	• **Floating Panel:** Edit Group • **Shortcut:** AD (when a group is in edit mode)
	Attached Detail Groups	• **Ribbon:** *Modify	Model Groups* tab>Group panel
	Create Group (Detail)	• **Ribbon:** *Annotate* tab>Detail panel, expand Detail Group • **Shortcut: GP**
	Create Group (elements selected)	• **Ribbon:** *Modify* contextual tab>Create panel • **Shortcut: GP**
	Create Group (Model)	• **Ribbon:** *Architecture* or *Structure* tab>Model panel, expand Model Group • **Shortcut: GP**

Button	Command	Location
	Edit Group	• **Ribbon:** *Modify	Model (or Detail) Groups* tab>Group panel • **Shortcut: EG** (when a group is selected)
	Load as Group	• **Ribbon:** *Insert* tab>Load from Library panel
	Load as Group into Open Projects	• **Ribbon:** *Architecture* or *Structure* tab>Model panel, expand Model Group
	Place Detail Group	• **Ribbon:** *Annotate* tab>Detail panel, expand Detail Group
	Place Model Group	• **Ribbon:** *Architecture* or *Structure* tab>Model panel, expand Model Group
	Remove from Group	• **Floating Panel:** Edit Group • **Shortcut: RG** (when a group is in edit mode)
	Ungroup	• **Ribbon:** *Modify	Model (or Detail) Groups* tab>Group panel • **Shortcut: UG** (when a group is selected)

Linking Models

Linking models in Revit® allows you to check for interferences in the design across multiple models, view information through a linked model, share information to any parties linking your model into theirs, and quickly identify or communicate design revisions. The Copy/Monitor tool will enable you to copy elements from a linked model into your own and will monitor them for any changes made to those elements in the original model so that you are alerted in the event of a revision.

Learning Objectives

- Link Revit models into a host project and manage the links.
- Modify link display settings in views.
- Copy and monitor elements from linked models.
- Use a coordination review to identify breaks in monitoring.
- Check interferences between elements in linked projects.

2.1 Linking Revit Models

You can link a Revit project into any other project. A linked model automatically updates if the original file is changed. This method can be used in many ways. For example, use this method when you have a number of identical buildings on one site plan, as shown in Figure 2–1. When you link one Revit model into another, the model that you are working in is called the *host* or *hosting* model, and the model that has been linked into the host model is called the *linked* model.

Figure 2–1

It is important to understand that when models are linked into a Revit project, that project remembers the paths so that the user does not have to relink the models every time they reopen their own model. This saves the user a great deal of time over the course of a project; however, it can also increase the amount of time it takes to open a model. The more linked models in a project, the longer it will take to open.

It is best practice, when linking models into one another, to use the same Revit version across all of the models.

Structural and MEP projects typically use the architectural model as the base for their projects, but there are times when an architect will link consultants' models into the architectural file as well.

* Architectural, structural, and MEP models created in the Revit can be linked to each other as long as they are from the same release cycle.

- When you use linked models, clashes between disciplines can be detected, and information can be passed between disciplines.

- Elements can be copied and monitored for even better coordination.

- Linked models can be constrained to elements in the host project and to each other. You can select references in linked models as a work plane and can schedule elements from the linked model in the host project.

Linking Revit models into other models is a common practice for many reasons and can provide a variety of benefits. The most common reasons to link one model into another are:

- Interdisciplinary coordination, such as linking an architectural model into a structural model to reference during the structural design process.

- Having multiple buildings on a single site, such as a college campus that has a variety of different buildings.

- Having identical buildings in multiple locations on a single site, such as an office park where the same building is used, but may be oriented differently.

- Having units that are used multiple times within a single project, such as patient rooms in a hospital, or multiple times across more than one project, such as a prototypical hotel guest room or lobby layout.

💡 Hint: Project Base Point

The origin of a project coordinate system is specified by the project base point, as shown in Figure 2–2. This should be set early in the project and before you start linking files together. It can be (but is not always) connected with the Survey Point, a secondary coordinate system used with shared coordinates. The internal origin, or startup location, never moves and is the internal coordinate system used for the base position for all of the model's elements.

Figure 2–2

- Project base points and survey points are visible in the Site view of the default architectural template. You can toggle them on in any view. In the Visibility/Graphic Overrides dialog box, in the *Model Category* tab, expand the **Site** category.

- The internal origin is typically off in all views, but it can be toggled on through the Visibility/Graphic Overrides dialog box, in the *Model Category* tab under the **Site** category.

- A linked model's project base, survey, and internal origin points will be grayed out in the view, indicating they belong to the linked model. The host model's points display in color, as shown in Figure 2–3.

Figure 2–3

- Spot coordinates and spot elevations are relative to the project base point.

How To: Link a Revit Model to a Host Project

1. In the *Insert* tab>Link panel, click 🔳 (Link Revit).

2. In the Import/Link RVT dialog box, select the file that you want to link. Before opening the file, set the *Positioning*, as shown in Figure 2–4, and click **Open**.

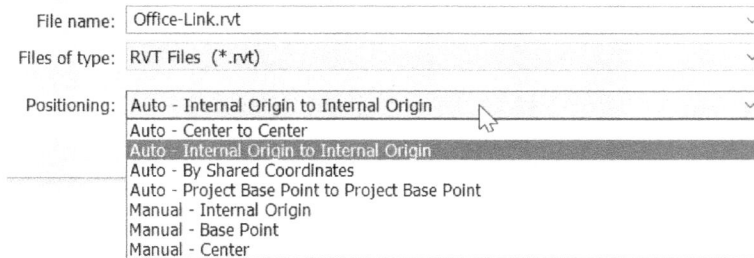

File name:	Office-Link.rvt
Files of type:	RVT Files (*.rvt)
Positioning:	Auto - Internal Origin to Internal Origin

Auto - Center to Center
Auto - Internal Origin to Internal Origin
Auto - By Shared Coordinates
Auto - Project Base Point to Project Base Point
Manual - Internal Origin
Manual - Base Point
Manual - Center

Figure 2–4

- Depending on how you decide to position the file, it is automatically placed in the file or you can manually place it with the cursor.

- The default positioning is **Auto - Internal Origin to Internal Origin**. The center of a linked model is the center of the geometry. Therefore, if you modify the extents of the original model, its exact location changes in the host project if you link **Center to Center**.

- **Auto - Project Base Point to Project Base Point** aligns the base points of the projects rather than the default origins.

- The software remembers the most recently used positioning type as long as you are in the same session of Revit. (The CAD Links dialog box remembers the last positioning used as well, but separately from RVT Links.)

- As the links are loading, do not click on the screen or click any buttons. The more links that are present in a project, the longer it takes to load.

- Linked models can be moved once you have placed them in the project. If you want to return them to the original location, right-click on the link and select either **Reposition to Project Base Point** or **Reposition to Internal Origin**, as shown in Figure 2–5.

Cancel

Repeat [Link Revit]

Recent Commands >

Reposition to Project Base Point

Reposition to Internal Origin

Figure 2–5

⚲ Hint: Preventing Linked Model from Being Moved

Once a linked model is in the correct location, you can lock it in place to ensure that it does not get moved by mistake, or prevent the linked model from being selected.

- To toggle off the ability to select links, in the Status Bar, click ⛀ (Select Links).
- To pin the linked model in place, select it and in the *Modify* tab>Modify panel, click ⛏ (Pin).
- To prevent pinned elements from being selected, in the Status Bar, click ⛏ (Select Pinned Elements).

Multiple Copies of Links

Copied instances of a linked model are typically used when creating a master project with the same building placed in multiple locations, such as a university campus with several identical student residences, or with identical units, such as hospital rooms used multiple times within one building.

- Linked models can be copied, rotated, arrayed, and mirrored.There is only one linked model, and any copies are additional instances of the link.
- Copies are numbered automatically. You can change their names in Properties when the instance is selected.
- When you have placed a link in a project, you can drag and drop additional copies of the link into the project from the Project Browser>**Revit Links** node, as shown in Figure 2−6.

Figure 2−6

Annotation and Linked Models

Many annotations can be added to the host model that reference elements in the linked model. For example, in Figure 2–7, the walls columns and grid lines are part of the linked model but the dimensions and tags are placed in the host project.

Figure 2–7

- Elements in the linked model can also be scheduled in the host project.

- The information annotated or scheduled for elements in a linked model cannot be controlled through the host model. Therefore, it is best to coordinate what information needs to be used in the hosting model annotation at the beginning of the project rather than waiting until it is necessary.

Managing Links

A linked model reloads each time the host project is opened. You can also reload the model by right-clicking on the Revit Link in the Project Browser, and then selecting **Reload** or **Reload From**, as shown in Figure 2–8.

Figure 2–8

The Manage Links dialog box (shown in Figure 2–9) enables you to reload, unload, add, and remove links. Additionally, it provides access to other options. To open the Manage Links dialog box, in the *Insert* tab>Link, panel click (Manage Links). The Manage Links dialog box also displays when you select a link in the *Modify | RVT Links* tab.

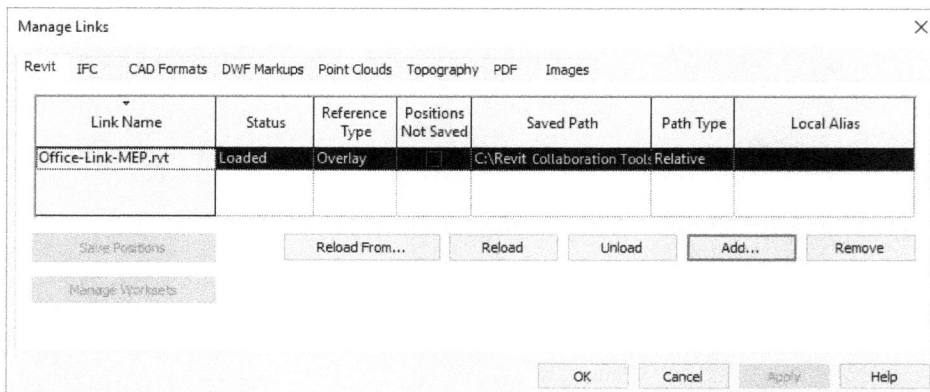

Figure 2–9

The options available in the Manage Links dialog box include the following:

- **Reload From:** Opens the Add Link dialog box, which enables you to select the file you want to reload. Use this if the linked file location or name has changed.

- **Reload:** Reloads the file without additional prompts.

- **Unload:** Unloads the file so that it the link is kept, but the file is not displayed or calculated in the project. Use **Reload** to restore it.

- **Add:** Opens the Import/Link RVT dialog box, which enables you to link additional models into the host project.

- **Remove:** Deletes the link from the file.

Links can be nested into one another. How a link responds when the host project is linked into another project depends on the option in the *Reference Type* column:

- **Overlay:** The nested linked model is not referenced in the new host project.

- **Attach:** The nested linked model displays in the new host project.

The option in the *Path Type* column controls how the location of the link is remembered:

- **Relative**

  - Searches the root folder of the current project.
  - If the file is moved, the software still searches for it.

- **Absolute**

  - Searches the entire file path where the file was originally saved.
  - If the original file is moved, the software is not able to find it.

- Other options control how the linked file interfaces with worksets and saved positioning.

- In the Manage Links dialog box, when you have multiple links, you can sort rows by clicking the column header.

Linked Model Properties

Linked models have both instance properties and type properties. Instance Properties, as shown in Figure 2–10, include the *Name* for the individual copy of the link. This is automatically updated as you insert more than one. You can also change the name to help you identify it later. It also shows if it is part of a *Design Option* and if it is set to a *Shared Site*.

Figure 2–10

Type Properties, as shown in Figure 2–11, include *Room Bounding* which is required if you want to be able to place rooms or spaces from the information in the linked model. It also includes *Reference Type* (Overlay or Attachment) and *Phase Mapping* as well as workset information if the project is workshared.

Figure 2–11

The phases in linked models can be mapped to the host project phasing so that the phasing schemes from different projects can be displayed consistently. Edit the Type Properties of the linked model and next to *Phase Mapping*, click **Edit...**. In the Phases dialog box, as shown in Figure 2–12, select the Phase from the linked model to match the corresponding phase in the host project.

Figure 2–12

Linked Model Conversion

There are times when you require information stored in a linked file that is brought into your host file. The information required might be about one or more individual elements or an entire link. A link can be converted to a group by binding it to the project. The group becomes a part of the project and does not update if the original file is modified. You can also convert a group to a link, which creates a new project file containing the elements of the group. Links and groups display differently when selected, as shown in Figure 2–13.

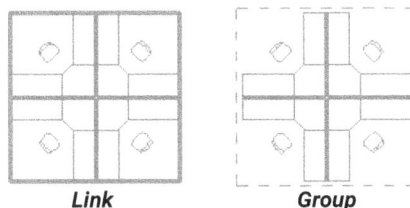

Link   *Group*

Figure 2–13

How To: Copy Individual Elements in a Linked File to the Host File

1. Select an individual element in a linked model by moving the cursor over the element and pressing <Tab>.

2. When the element you want to use highlights, click on it.

3. In the *Modify | RVT Links* tab>Clipboard panel, click 📄 (Copy to the Clipboard).

4. Click 📋 (Paste from Clipboard) to insert the individual element into the project, as shown in Figure 2−14.

    Note: Individual items in a linked model can be copied into the host project or into another project file.

Link   **Individual Element Copied**

Figure 2−14

*   This is not the same as copying and monitoring elements.

How To: Convert a Link to a Group

1. Select the link. In the *Modify | RVT Links* tab>Link panel, click 📋 (Bind Link).

2. The Bind Link Options dialog box opens, as shown in Figure 2−15. Select the items that you want to include and click **OK**.

Figure 2−15

- An alert box might open, warning you about duplicate types. The types in the current project override the types in the linked project.

- If there is an existing group with the same name as the link in the project, an alert box opens, as shown in Figure 2–16.

Figure 2–16

How To: Convert Groups to Links

1. Select the group(s) you want to convert. You can select multiple copies, but they must be the same group.
2. In the *Modify | Model Groups* tab>Group panel, click [icon] (Link).
3. In the Convert to Link dialog box, select the method for converting the group, as shown in Figure 2–17.

Figure 2–17

4. When you select **Replace with a new project file,** the Save Group dialog box displays. Navigate to the appropriate folder, name the group (the default is the same as the group name), and click **Save**.

   - Select **Include attached detail groups as views** when you have both a model group and detail group together.

5. When you select **Replace with an existing project file,** the Open dialog box displays. Navigate to the appropriate folder, select the file you want to use to replace the selected group and click **Open**.

2.2 Views and Linked Models

Linked files can be very large and include a lot of information that is not required when all you want is the base building model. Depending on the standards of your office, it can help to clean up the linked file by deleting unnecessary views or sheets and purging out all unused families. If required, you can request the original creator to set up coordination views that can be used specifically as a base view in the project.

Preparing Views for Other Disciplines

If you are working with consultants from other disciplines, it can be helpful to create coordination views for them that include only the element types that they require. For example, in Figure 2–18, the architect created plans for the first and second floors as a base for MEP and Structural projects. These views display only the architectural elements that other disciplines require as a background for their own elements.

Figure 2–18

- When a model is linked to a host project, any changes you make in the Visibility/Graphic Overrides dialog box are also made in the linked model by default. For example, if you toggle off the visibility of the grid lines in the host project, it also toggles off the visibility of the grid lines in linked models.

Individual elements in linked models can be hidden in the host project as shown in Figure 2–19. To select an element in a linked model, hover the cursor over the element and press <Tab> until only that element highlights. Then, right-click and select **Hide in View> Elements**. You can do this in plans, sections, elevations, and 3D views.

Three instances of a linked model with the chair hidden in one instance

Figure 2–19

- You can only modify the graphic overrides of elements in linked models by category, not by element.
- Hiding elements in the linked model By Category, has the same effect as hiding elements By category in the Main Model. All elements of that category are hidden in the Main Model and in all instances of all links, unless other link(s) have overrides attached to them.

Temporary View Properties

As you are working, it can be helpful to temporarily override the view. You can do this by selecting a view template from the View Control Bar, as shown in Figure 2–20.

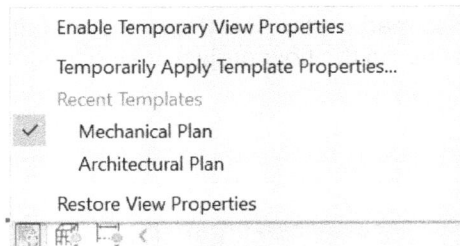

Figure 2–20

How To: Temporarily Override the View Properties

1. In the View Control Bar, expand 🔲 (Temporary View Properties) and select **Enable Temporary View Properties**.

2. Expand 🔲 (Temporary View Properties) again and select **Temporarily Apply Template Properties**.

   - Alternatively, if you have already used the process, you can select from a list of view templates, as shown previously in Figure 2–20.

3. In the Temporarily Apply Template Properties dialog box, select the view template you want to apply and click **OK**.

4. When ready to return to the original view properties, expand 🔲 (Temporary View Properties) and select **Restore View Properties**.

Some companies create a "working view" template to be used as a temporary override, rather than having separate working views.

Display Settings in Linked Models

To further customize views in projects with links, you can modify the Display Settings of the link. By default, the link displays using the host view parameters, but you can change it to use a view in the linked file or a custom view where you can specify every aspect of its appearance.

For example, in Figure 2–21, an MEP model has been linked into an architectural model and the Display Settings are set to **By Host View**. Only a couple of MEP elements display by default, such as the lights and some piping.

*Note: If a graphic override has been applied to categories in a project, the linked files are also modified if their display setting is set to **By host view**.*

Figure 2–21

In Figure 2–22, the Display Settings have been changed to **By Linked View** with a mechanical view selected. The duct work and air terminals display, the lights remain grayed out and piping is toggled off.

Figure 2–22

In Figure 2–23, the Display Settings have been customized. The Mechanical view is still selected but all of the duct elements are toggled off while the air terminals display.

Figure 2–23

How To: Modify Display Settings in a Linked View

1. Type **VV** or **VG** to open the Visibility/Graphic Overrides dialog box.

2. Switch to the *Revit Links* tab.

3. Set the *Display Settings* for the linked model or an instance of the linked model, as shown in Figure 2–24.

   Note: If you have more than one copy of a link, you can have them all update together by clicking on the Display Settings next to the link name rather than the instance name.

Figure 2–24

4. In the RVT Link Display Settings dialog box, in the *Basics* tab, select **By linked view** or **Custom**.

• If you select **By linked view**, you can select from a list of views in the linked model, as shown in Figure 2–25.

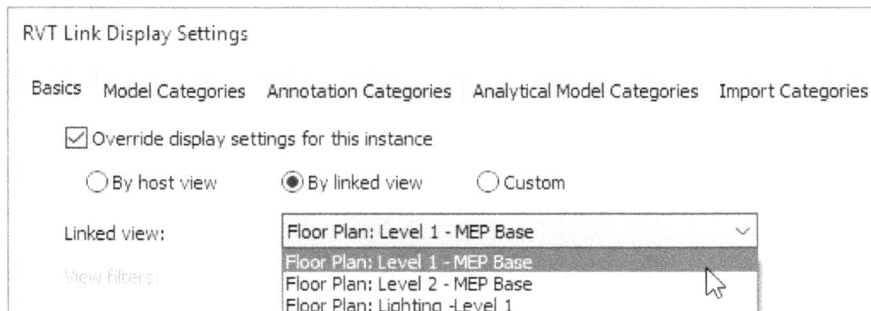

Figure 2–25

- If you select **Custom**, you can specify each setting independently, as shown in Figure 2–26.

Figure 2–26

- When **Custom** is selected, you can also customize the display of specific categories using other tabs in the RVT Link Display Settings dialog box.

- If a linked model contains phases that are not in the host project, they can still be displayed by overriding the display settings for that instance of the linked model. The phases from the linked model display in the Phase drop-down list.

Practice 2a
Link Models - All Disciplines

Practice Objectives

* Link several models into a host project.
* Make copies of linked models in a project.
* Modify the Visibility/Graphic Overrides of the copied links.

In this practice, you will link architectural, structural, and MEP models into a host building site project. You will make copies of the linked models and modify the Visibility/Graphic Overrides for several of the instances. You will also modify one of the linked models and then reopen the site model to see how the changes automatically update in the final project, as shown in Figure 2–27.

| Architectural | Structural | Lighting |

Figure 2–27

Task 1: Link several models into a host project.

1. In the practice files *General* folder, open **Industrial-Park-M.rvt**. The site has six rectangular pads for warehouse buildings.
2. In the *Insert* tab>Link panel, click 🅡 (Link Revit).
3. In the Import/Link RVT dialog box, select the file **Arch-Building-M.rvt** from the practice files *General>Links* folder. Verify that the *Positioning* is set to **Auto - Internal Origin to Internal Origin**.
4. Click **Open**.

   Note: The building does not line up properly with any pad. This will be corrected later.

5. Select the new link. In Properties, verify that the *Name* of this instance is **1**. This makes tracking the rest of the instances easier.

6. Click ![Link Revit icon] (Link Revit) again and link in **MEP-Building-M.rvt** from the practice files *General> Links* folder, at the same position.

   • An alert box opens, warning you that the model has another model linked to it and that it is not visible in this project. This is because it was linked in that file as an overlay rather than an attachment. Close the alert box.

7. Repeat the process one more time and link in **Struct-Building-M.rvt** from the practice files *General>Links* folder, at the same position. The Nested Links Invisible alert box opens again because of the overlay. Close the alert box.

8. The buildings need to be moved to the correct location. Select all of the linked models that are on top of each other and move them to one of the pads at the top of the site. You might need to zoom in to place it precisely. Hint: Use the snap shortcut **SE** to snap to the end.

   *Note: When selecting the three linked models, use the **Filter** command to filter out any unnecessary elements.*

9. Copy the linked models to the other top two pads on the same side of the parking lot.

10. Draw reference planes and dimensions to find the middle of the north and south building pads, as shown in Figure 2–28.

Figure 2–28

11. Select the three buildings along the top, then use **Filter** to filter out just the RVT links. Start the **Mirror** command and select **Copy** from the Options Bar. Mirror the links from the top north building pads to the bottom south building pads. Verify they are sitting on top of the building pads and move them into place, if needed, as shown in Figure 2–29.

Figure 2–29

12. Save the project.

Task 2: Modify the Visibility/Graphic Overrides of the links.

1. Zoom in to see the top three warehouses.

2. Type **VV** to open the Visibility/Graphic Overrides dialog box. In the *Revit Links* tab, next to the main MEP and Structural links, select **Halftone**. Click **Apply** and move the dialog box out of the way slightly so that you can see the changes, as shown in Figure 2–30.

Figure 2–30

3. Remain in the Visibility/Graphic Overrides dialog box, *Revit Links* tab. Set up the first pad location so that it displays the architectural information, as shown in Figure 2–31. Expand the lists beside each of the links and clear the first instance of MEP (2) and Structural (3) links. Click **Apply**. Only the architectural information displays in this one instance

4. Set up the second pad location to display only the structural information, as shown in Figure 2–31. Clear the second architectural instance (4) and the second MEP instance (5). Click **Apply**. Only the structural information displays in this instance.

5. Set up the third pad location to display the MEP lighting information. Clear the third architectural (7) and structural (9) instances. Click **Apply**. Not enough information displays in this instance, as shown in the bottom image in Figure 2–31.

Figure 2–31

6. Check the checkbox for the third architectural instance (7) to turn it back on again and change only this one instance to **Halftone**, as shown in Figure 2–32.

7. Clear the **Halftone** option for the main MEP link.

8. Click **Not Overridden** in the *Display Settings* column for the third MEP instance (8), as shown in Figure 2–32.

Figure 2–32

9. In the RVT Link Display Settings dialog box, in the *Basics* tab, select **Override display settings for this instance**. Select the **By linked view** option and verify that the *Linked view* is set to **Floor Plan: 1 - Lighting**, as shown in Figure 2–33.

Figure 2–33

10. Click **OK** twice to close the dialog boxes.

11. Zoom in to see the lighting layout in the office area, as shown in Figure 2−34.

Figure 2−34

12. Save and close the project.

Task 3: Modify linked models.

1. Open **Arch-Building-M.rvt** from your practice files *General>Links* folder.

2. Add additional interior walls and doors to the office area of the warehouse, similar to the circled area in Figure 2−35.

Figure 2−35

3. Duplicate the **Floor Plan: Level 1** view and rename it to **Level 1 - Coordination**. Verify that the tags and grid lines are not displaying, as shown above in Figure 2-35.

4. Save and close the project.

5. Open **MEP-Building-M.rvt** from your practice files *General>Links* folder. The linked architectural model is automatically updated in this project.

6. Open the Electrical>Lighting>**Ceiling Plans: 1 - Ceiling Elec** view.

7. Depending on where you added walls, modify the lighting locations.

8. Save and close the file.

9. Reopen the project **Industrial-Park-M.rvt**. The new walls and the modified lighting locations display in the linked files, as shown in Figure 2-36 for the office section at the third pad location.

Figure 2-36

10. Type **VV** and for the third architectural instance (7), override the Display Settings by linked view. Select **Floor Plan: Level 1 - Coordination**. The grid lines no longer display in this instance.

11. Save and close the project.

12. If you have time, you can link the structural model into the architectural model and delete the columns and extra grid lines because the structural model uses a wide-span structural system.

13. In the structural model, you can also add more beams and other structural elements to finish the project. Test it in the Industrial Park project.

End of practice

2.3 Copying and Monitoring Elements

When working with linked files, such as an architectural model linked into a structural or MEP project, you can coordinate information between the files using the **Copy/Monitor** tool. When you monitor an item in the linked file with an identical or similar one in the host project, the program tracks these two items, looking for changes in location, existence, height, etc. It always requires two elements to compare.

Items that are monitored display the ⌁ icon when selected, as shown in Figure 2–37.

> *Note: Copy/Monitor works with grid lines, levels, columns, walls, and floors, as well as MEP fixtures in the same file or in a linked file.*

Figure 2–37

When starting the Copy/Monitor command, you can choose **Use Current Project** or **Select Link**. Use Select Link to monitor a linked file's elements if they could potentially be moved and affect your system.

*   **Copy:** Copies the selected element from the linked model to the current model or host model, then monitors the element for any changes that may happen in the linked model.

*   **Monitor:** Compares two elements of the same type against each other, either from a linked model to the current project (as shown in Figure 2–38) or in the current project.

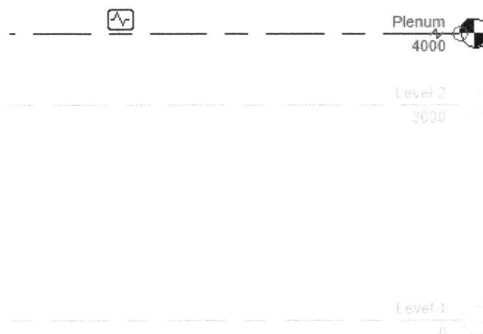

Figure 2–38

What Is Typically Copied/Monitored?

* **Architecture:** The **Copy/Monitor** tool is not heavily used by architects, although they might on occasion monitor elements in their project. For some projects they might use the structural engineer's linked model to control the grid lines and column locations or the plumbing engineer's linked model to control the location of the plumbing fixtures.

* **Structure:** Structural consultants copy/monitor levels, grid lines, columns, floors, and bearing walls from the architectural project.

* **MEP:** Mechanical consultants monitor levels and grid lines from the architectural model. They also copy/monitor some elements including plumbing and lighting fixtures.

* It is especially important to agree who controls datum elements, such as levels and grid lines, and not to modify them without explicit communication with others using that project as a link.

How To: Copy and Monitor Elements from a Linked File

1. In the *Collaborate* tab>Coordinate panel, expand (Copy/Monitor) and click (Select Link).

2. Select the link.

3. In the *Copy/Monitor* tab>Tools panel, click (Copy) or (Monitor).

4. If copying from the linked file, select each element that you want to copy. Alternatively, use the **Multiple** option:

   * In the Options Bar, select **Multiple**, as shown in Figure 2−39.

Figure 2−39

   * Hold <Ctrl> and select the elements that you want to copy into your model individually, or use a pick and drag window around multiple elements.

   Note: Warnings about duplicated or renamed types might display.

   * In the Options Bar, click **Finish**.

* If monitoring elements in the current project with elements in the linked model, first select the element in the current project and then select the element in the linked model.

5. Click (Finish) to end the session of Copy/Monitor.

How To: Copy and Monitor Elements in the Current Project

1. In the *Collaborate* tab>Coordinate panel, expand (Copy/Monitor) and click (Use Current Project).

2. In the *Copy/Monitor* tab>Tools panel, click (Copy) or (Monitor).

3. Select the two elements you want to monitor.

4. Repeat the process for any additional elements.

5. Click (Finish) to end the command.

- The elements do not have to be at the same elevation or location for the software to monitor them.

Copy/Monitor Options

Before starting the copy/monitor process, you can modify settings for the types of elements. In the *Copy/Monitor* tab>Tools panel, click (Options). In the Copy/Monitor Options dialog box, select the tab for the type of element that you want to copy: *Levels*, *Grids*, *Columns*, *Walls*, or *Floors*, as shown in Figure 2–40.

> *Note: Tabs display for the categories that exist in the linked project.*

Figure 2–40

- By default, hosted elements such as shaft openings in floors and door, and window openings in walls (as shown in Figure 2–41) are automatically copied with their host elements. You can change this response in the Copy/Monitor Options dialog box, in the *Floors* tab *Additional Copy Parameters* area, as shown previously in Figure 2–40.

Figure 2–41

- MEP projects have additional options for Coordination Settings where you specify the copy and mapping behavior for different HVAC, Plumbing, Electrical equipment and fixtures, and other related devices, as shown in Figure 2–42. These elements can also be batch copied into the host project from the linked model.

Figure 2–42

💡 Hint: Start a New Project from a Revit Template File

1. In the *File* tab, expand ⬜ (New) and click ⬛ (Project) (as shown in Figure 2–43), or press <Ctrl>+<N>.

Figure 2–43

2. In the New Project dialog box (shown in Figure 2–44), select the template that you want to use and click **OK**.

• Click **Browse...** to browse to the Revit templates or to a custom template, if needed.

Figure 2–44

• The list of template files is set in the Options dialog box in the *File Locations* pane. It might vary depending on the installed product and company standards.

• You can select from a list of templates if they have been set up by your BIM manager.

2.4 Coordinating Linked Models

Monitoring elements identifies changes in the data and changes in placement. For example, if you move a grid line, a Coordination Monitor alert displays, as shown in Figure 2–45. You can run a coordination review to correct or accept these changes.

Figure 2–45

- If you open a project with a linked file containing elements that have been modified and monitored, the warning dialog box shown in Figure 2–46 displays.

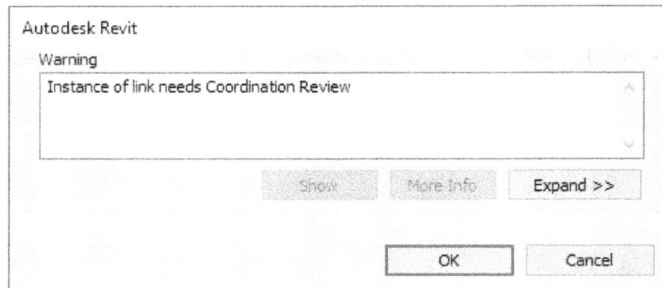

Figure 2–46

- Warnings do not prevent you from making a change, but rather alert you that the element is monitored and requires further coordination.

- If you no longer want an element to be monitored, select it and in the associated *Modify* tab>Monitor panel, click ![icon] (Stop Monitoring).

- When you work in a host project and move an element that is copied into the host file, a warning displays as shown above in Figure 2–45. This does not prevent you from making the change, but alerts you that this is a monitored element that requires further coordination with the other disciplines involved.

- If you make a change to a monitored host element, such as adding a door in a wall, a warning opens as shown in Figure 2−47.

Warning

Coordination Monitor alert : New Openings Detected in 'Basic Wall : WT-04'

Figure 2−47

How To: Run a Coordination Review

1. In the *Collaborate* tab>Coordinate panel, expand ⬡ (Coordination Review) and click ⬡ (Use Current Project) or ⬡ (Select Link). The Coordination Review dialog box lists any conflicts detected, as shown in Figure 2−48.

   - If there are no conflicts, the *Message* area is empty.

Figure 2−48

2. Use the Group by: drop-down list to group the information by **Status, Category**, and **Rule** in a variety of different ways. This is important if you have many elements to review.

3. Select an *Action* for each conflict related to the elements involved, as shown in Figure 2–49.

Figure 2–49

- **Postpone:** Do nothing, but leave it to be handled later.

- **Reject:** Do not accept the change. The change needs to be made in the other model.

- **Accept Difference:** Make no change to the monitored element in the current project, but accept the change (such as a distance between the elements) in the monitor status.

- **Rename/Modify/Move:** Apply the change to the monitored element.

- Other options display when special cases occur. For more information, see the Autodesk Revit help files.

4. Add a comment by clicking **Add comment** in the column to the right. This enables you to make a note about the change, such as the date of the modification.

5. Select the element names or click **Show** to display any items in conflict. Clicking **Show** changes the view to center the elements in your screen. Selecting the name does not change the view.

6. Click **Create Report** to create an HTML report that you can share with other users, as shown in Figure 2–50.

Revit Coordination Report

In host project

New/Unresolved	Plumbing Fixtures	Maintain relative position of Fixtures	Relative position of two Fixtures changed	Plumbing Fixtures : Sink_Kitchen-Single[1] : Mark 1 : id 734856 MEP-Elementary-School-Architectural.rvt : Plumbing Fixtures : Sink_Kitchen-Single[1] : Mark 80 : id 329165

Figure 2–50

Reconciling Hosts

If the owner of a linked file deletes or moves a host, such as a wall and the current project had elements hosted to it, such as a light fixture, the connection between the two is lost, as shown in Figure 2–51.

Figure 2–51

How To: Reconcile Hosting

1. When you open a project or reload a linked file, an alert box might be displayed, as shown in Figure 2–52.

Figure 2–52

2. In the *Collaborate* tab>Coordinate panel, click (Reconcile Hosting). The Reconcile Hosting palette displays (shown in Figure 2–53).

3. Expand the list, select the element, and click **Show** to zoom in on the element that is orphaned.

4. To correct the issue, right-click on the element name, as shown in Figure 2–53, and select **Pick Host** or **Delete**.

Reconcile Hosting

| Graphics | Sort | Show |

- Orphaned Elements (1)
  - Industrial-Building-A.rvt : 1 : location <N
    - Lighting Fixtures (1)
      - Lighting

        Pick Host

        Delete

Figure 2–53

- You can also select the element and in the *Modify* contextual tab>Work Plane panel, click

  (Pick New) and select a new host or delete it.

5. When you are finished correcting the elements, close the Reconcile Hosting palette.

- If you have control of the host elements in your project and you want to use a different wall type, do not delete and redraw the wall, just select it and in the Type Selector, select the new type. This does not create issues for others who are using the model as a link which has objects hosted on it.

- Because of this issue, many hosted elements are face-based rather than wall (or other host type) based. These elements do not notify you if a host is moved so you need to be aware to look for these orphaned elements.

Interference Checking

Interference Checking can be used when there are potential overlaps between disciplines, such as the structural column and ducts shown in Figure 2–54.

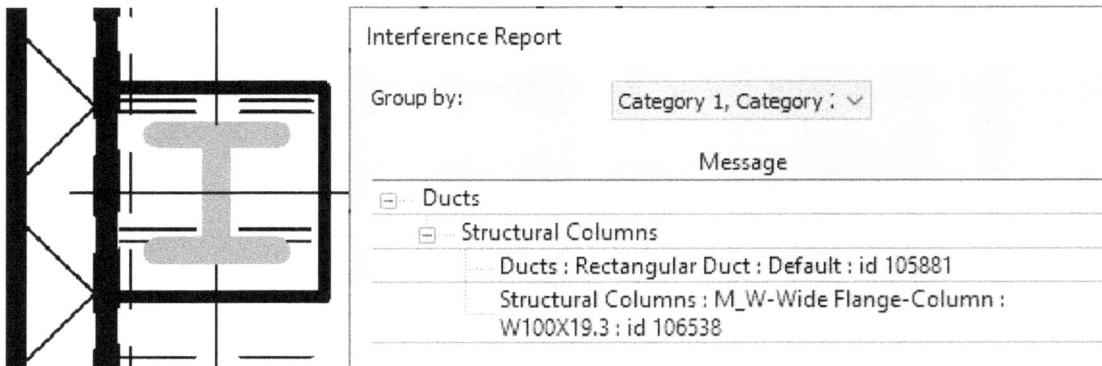

Interference Report

Group by: Category 1, Category : ∨

Message

- Ducts
  - Structural Columns
    - Ducts : Rectangular Duct : Default : id 105881
    - Structural Columns : M_W-Wide Flange-Column : W100X19.3 : id 106538

Figure 2–54

- Typical items to check include structural elements against architectural columns, walls, door or window openings, floors and roofs, specialty equipment and floors, and any elements in a linked file with the host file.

- For more complex projects and those that include files from other software, the Navisworks software provides a much more powerful solution than this basic interference checking.

How To: Run an Interference Check

1. In the *Collaborate* tab>Coordinate panel, expand ▣ (Interference Check) and click

   ▣ (Run Interference Check).

   - To filter out unneeded elements, select the elements first and then run the interference check.

2. In the Interference Check dialog box, as shown in Figure 2−55, in the *Categories from* drop-down list, select the projects that you want to compare. This can be the same project or any linked projects.

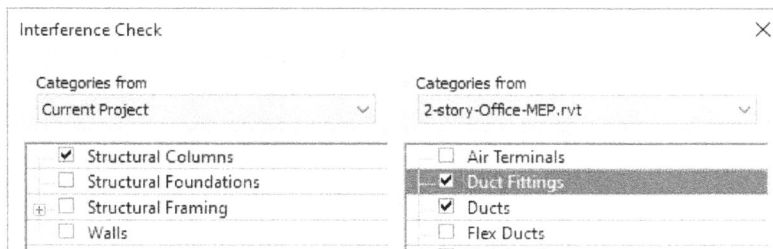

Figure 2−55

3. Select the element types that you want to compare.

   Note: Select only the categories that you need to review. In a large project, selecting all categories can take a very long time to process.

4. Click **OK**.

5. If there are interferences, the Interference Report dialog box opens, as shown in Figure 2–56.

Interference Report

Group by: Category 1, Category : ⌄

Message

⊟ Ducts
      ⊟ Structural Columns
           Ducts : Rectangular Duct : Default : id 105881
           Structural Columns : M_W-Wide Flange-Column : id 106538

Created: Thursday, October 24, 2019 12:57:01 PM
Last Update:

Note: Refresh updates interferences listed above.

| Show | Export... | Refresh | Close |

Figure 2–56

6. To see the elements that are interfering, select an element in the list and click **Show**.

7. If you need to create a report that can be viewed by other users, click **Export...**. This creates an HTML file listing the conflicts.

8. The dialog box can remain open while you make changes or you can click **Close** and then expand 🔲⌄ (Interference Check) and click 🔲 (Show Last Report) to see the report again.

9. In the Interference Report dialog box, click **Refresh** to display any changes.

10. Refreshing the report only reviews the elements selected when the report was first run. If you need to select other elements, run a new report.

Practice 2b
Coordinate Linked Projects - Structural

Practice Objectives

- Link in an architectural project.
- Copy and monitor elements.
- Modify the architectural project.
- Review and correct issues when coordination relationships established with Copy/Monitor are broken.

In this practice, you will start a new structural project and link in an architectural model. You will then Copy/Monitor the grid lines, set up Column options to use structural columns, and Copy/Monitor in the columns, as shown in Figure 2–57. Finally, you will make changes to the architectural project and then use Coordination Review to match the structural project with the link.

Figure 2–57

- It is recommended that you complete both Practice 2b and Practice 2c, if time permits, even if they are not for your specific discipline. The principles involved in these practices are the same for all disciplines.

Task 1: Link a file and copy/monitor elements.

1. Start a new project. In the New Project dialog box, browse to the practice files *Templates* folder. Select **Metric-Structural Template.rte** and click **Open**.

2. In the New Project dialog box, click **OK**.

3. Save the project as **Struct-Warehouse-M.rvt** in your practice files *Structural* folder.

4. Open the **Structural Plans: Level 1** view.

5. In the *Insert* tab>Link panel, click 🔲 (Link Revit).

6. In the Import/Link RVT dialog box, navigate to the practice files *Structural>Links* folder and select **Arch-Warehouse-M.rvt**. Verify that the *Positioning* is set to **Auto - Internal Origin to Internal Origin** and click **Open**.

*   The columns, grid lines, and foundation elements of the linked model display, while the walls do not because they are not structural.

7. In the View Control Bar, click 🔲 (Temporary View Properties) and select **Temporarily Apply Template Properties**.

8. In the Temporarily Apply Template Properties dialog box select **Architectural Plan** and click **OK**.

9. In the *Collaborate* tab>Coordinate panel, expand 🔲 (Copy/Monitor) and click 🔲 (Select Link).

10. Select the linked warehouse model.

11. In the *Copy/Monitor* tab>Tools panel, click 🔲 (Copy).

12. In the Options Bar, select **Multiple**. Select all of the grid lines using any selection method, such as that shown in Figure 2–58. Hold <Ctrl> to select additional grid lines, if needed. In the Options Bar, click **Finish**.

Figure 2–58

*   Read and close any warning messages that appear.

13. The grid lines are copied into the host project and monitored in place, as shown in Figure 2–59.

Figure 2–59

14. Click **Modify** to release the grid lines.

   • Read and close any warning messages that appear.

15. Return to the *Copy/Monitor* tab. In the Tools panel, click ✎ (Options).

16. In the Copy/Monitor Options dialog box, select the *Columns* tab. The types of columns in the linked file are listed on the left. Verify that the architectural columns are set to a structural column type. For the *Pipe-Column*, select **Copy original Type** as shown in Figure 2–60.

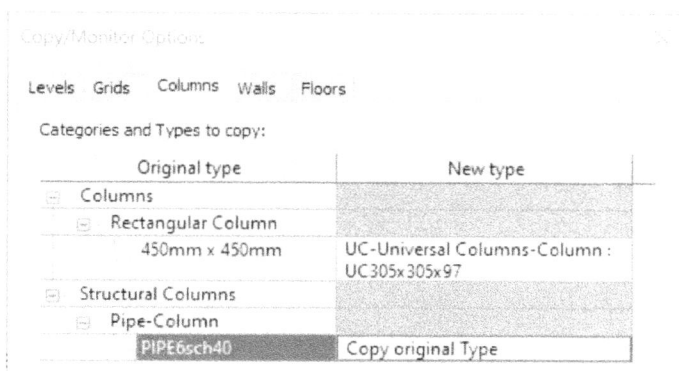

Figure 2–60

17. Click **OK**.

18. In the *Copy/Monitor* tab>Tools panel, click ⊙ (Copy).

19. In the Options Bar, select **Multiple**.

20. Create a window around the entire building to select everything but the grid lines.

21. In the Status Bar or Options Bar, click ▽ (Filter).

22. In the Filter dialog box, select only the **Columns** and **Structural Columns** and click **OK**.

23. In the Options Bar, click **Finish**.

24. The columns are copied into the project as shown in Figure 2–61.

  • Read and close any warning messages that appear.

Figure 2–61

25. In the *Copy/Monitor* tab, click ✔ (Finish).

26. Zoom into the columns. There should be structural columns at the location of the square architectural columns, as shown in Figure 2–62, and pipe columns in the center of the building.

Figure 2–62

27. Save and close the project.

Task 2: Modify the architectural project.

1. Open **Arch-Warehouse-M.rvt** from your practice files *Structural>Links* folder.

2. Zoom in to check that there are no structural columns where the architectural columns are, as shown in Figure 2–63.

Figure 2–63

3. Zoom out.

4. Select grid line 3 and change it so it is **3700mm** from grid line 2, as shown in Figure 2–64.

   Note: Use the temporary dimensions to help you by moving the witness lines.

Figure 2–64

5. Repeat the process with grid line 5 and move it **3700mm** from grid line 6. The associated architectural columns move with the grid line.

6. Save and close the project.

Task 3: Coordinate the host file with the linked file.

1. Open the project **Struct-Warehouse-M.rvt** that you created earlier. The warning about needing a coordination review displays, as shown in Figure 2–65.

Figure 2–65

2. Click **OK**.

3. Set the *Temporary View Properties* to **Architectural Plan**, as shown in Figure 2–66.

Figure 2–66

4. You can see the change between the host project and linked model, as shown in Figure 2−67.

Figure 2−67

5. In the *Collaborate* tab> Coordinate panel, expand ![icon] (Coordination Review) and click ![icon] (Select Link).

6. Select the linked model.

7. In the Coordination Review dialog box, review the issues by expanding the nodes, as shown in Figure 2–68.

8. In the *Action* column, next to the first *Grid moved* issue, select **Modify Grid '5'** and set the second *Grid moved* issue to **Modify Grid '3'**, as shown in Figure 2–68.

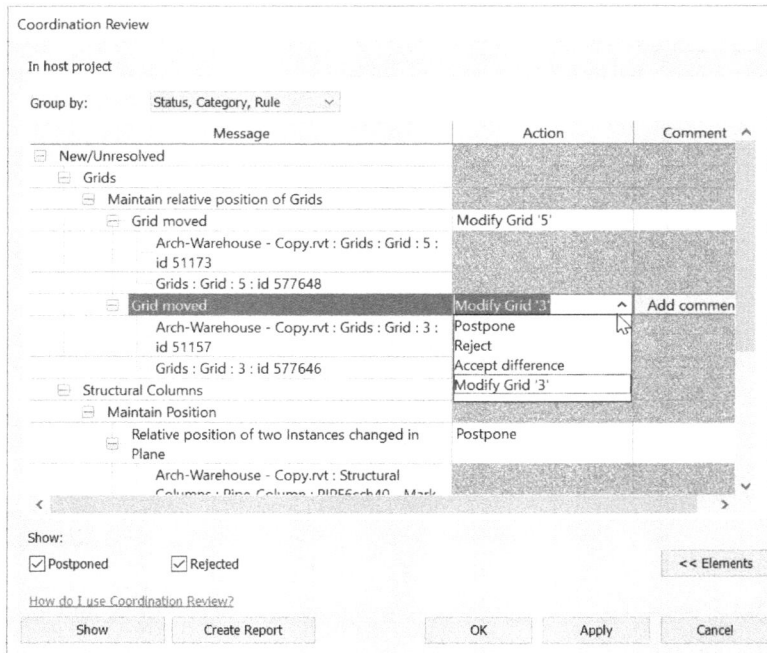

Figure 2–68

9. Click **Apply**. The grid lines move over, and because columns move with grid lines, the issues with the structural columns are resolved and are not listed in the Coordination Review dialog box.

10. Click **OK** and the host file matches up with the linked file.

11. Save and close the project.

End of practice

Practice 2c
Coordinate Linked Projects - MEP

Practice Objectives

- Link in an architectural project.
- Copy and monitor elements.
- Modify the architectural project.
- Review and correct issues when coordination relationships established with Copy/ Monitor are broken.

In this practice, you will create a new systems project and link in an architectural model. You will then use Copy/Monitor to monitor levels and draw some ductwork that references one of the levels as shown on the top in Figure 2–69. Finally, you will change the level in the architectural model and use Coordination Review to update the change in the systems model, as shown on the bottom in Figure 2–69.

Figure 2–69

- It is recommended that you complete both Practice 2b and Practice 2c, if time permits, even if they are not for your specific discipline. The principles involved in these practices are the same for all disciplines.

Task 1: Link a file and copy/monitor elements.

1. Start a new project. In the New Project dialog box, browse to the practice files *Templates* folder. Select **Metric-System Template.rte** and click **Open**.

2. In the New Project dialog box, click **OK**.

3. Save the project as **Mech-Warehouse-M.rvt** in your practice files *MEP* folder.

4. In the *Insert* tab>Link panel, click 🔲 (Link Revit).

5. In the Import/Link RVT dialog box, navigate to the practice files *MEP>Links* folder and select **Arch-Warehouse-M.rvt**. Verify that the *Positioning* is set to **Auto - Internal Origin to Internal Origin** and click **Open**.

6. Open the Mechanical>HVAC>**Elevations (Building Elevation): South - Mech** view. The host project has two levels and the architectural model has three, as shown in Figure 2–70. Hint: Select the linked file in the view and everything in the linked model will turn blue.

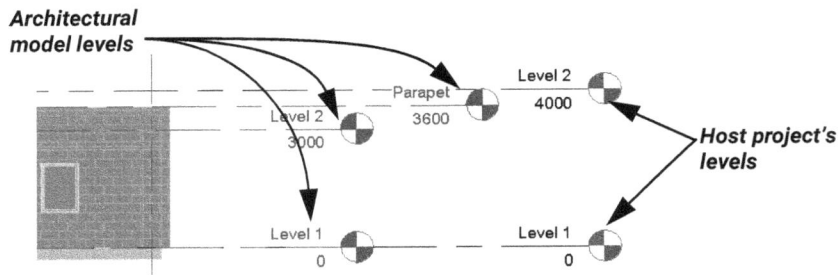

Figure 2–70

7. Change **Level 2** of the host project to **3000mm** to match with Level 2 of the linked project.

*Note: If you use the Align tool, make sure to uncheck **Lock** from the Align panel.*

8. In the *Collaborate* tab>Coordinate panel, expand 〽 (Copy/Monitor) and click 📄 (Select Link).

9. Select the linked warehouse model.

10. In the *Copy/Monitor* tab>Tools panel, click 〽 (Monitor).

11. Select Level 1 in the host project and then Level 1 in the linked model.

12. Repeat the process with Level 2 and click ✔ (Finish).

Task 2: Add ductwork.

1. Open the Mechanical>HVAC>Floor Plans>**1 - Mech** view.

2. In the *Systems* tab>HVAC panel, click 🖬 (Duct).

3. In Properties, set the *Reference Level* to **Level 2** and the *Middle Elevation* to (negative) -**3000mm**. Draw several ducts.

4. Return to the elevation view to see the location of the ducts, as shown in Figure 2−71.

Figure 2−71

5. Save and close the project.

Task 3: Modify the architectural project.

1. Open **Arch-Warehouse-M.rvt** from your practice files *MEP>Links* folder.

2. Open the **Elevations: South** view.

3. Change the height of Level 2 to **4000mm**.

   • The parapet level automatically changes height because it has been dimensioned and locked to Level 2.

4. Save and close the project.

Task 4: Coordinate the host file with the linked file.

1. Open the project **Mech-Warehouse-M.rvt** that you created earlier. The warning about needing a coordination review displays, as shown in Figure 2−72.

Figure 2−72

2. Click **OK**.

3. You can see the change between the host project and linked model as shown in Figure 2–73.

Figure 2–73

4. In the *Collaborate* tab> Coordinate panel, expand ⬚ (Coordination Review) and click ⬚ (Select Link).

5. Select the architectural link.

6. In the Coordination Review dialog box, expand the options in the *Action* column and select **Move Level 'Level 2'**, as shown in Figure 2–74.

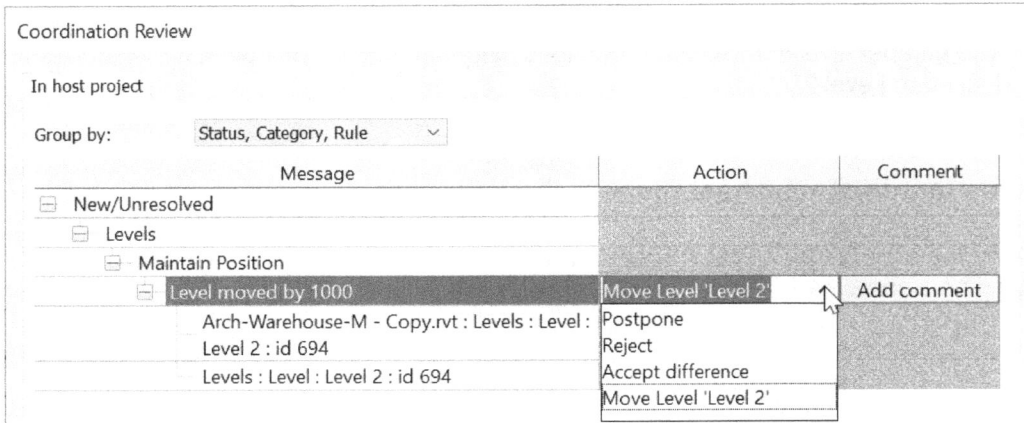

Figure 2–74

7. Click **OK** and the host file matches up with the linked file. The duct work moves as well because it was referenced to the level that was changed.

8. Save and close the project.

End of practice

Chapter Review Questions

1. When linking a Revit model into another project, which of the positioning methods keeps the model in the same place if the extents of the linked model changes in size?

    a. Auto - Center to Center

    b. Auto - Internal Origin to Internal Origin

    c. Manual - Base Point

    d. Manual - Center

2. If you want to toggle off all the grid lines in a linked file but still display them in the host file, what do you need to do?

    a. Select one of the grid lines in the linked file and select **Hide in View>Category**.

    b. Select one of the grid lines in the host file and, in the View Control Bar, expand ⚭ (Temporary Hide/Isolate) and select **Isolate Category**.

    c. In the Visibility/Graphic Overrides dialog box, change the link's *Display Settings* to **Custom** and in the *Annotation Categories* tab, clear **Grids**.

    d. In the Visibility/Graphic Overrides dialog box, in the *Annotation Categories* tab, clear **Grids**.

3. Which of the following elements, as shown in Figure 2−75, can be copied and monitored? (Select all that apply.)

    Figure 2−75

    a. Grid lines

    b. Walls

    c. Columns

    d. Doors

4. When working with nested links, which of the following describes the Reference Type that is NOT included when its host project is linked into another project?

    a. Attach

    b. Bind

    c. Import

    d. Overlay

5. What type of element(s) is created when you bring links permanently into a host file?

    a. The elements come in individually

    b. A block

    c. A group

    d. An import

6. When working with a linked file, as shown in Figure 2–76, what property do you need to set to be able to add rooms or spaces?

Figure 2–76

    a. Reference Type

    b. Room Bounding

    c. Phase Mapping

    d. Shared Site

7. In Figure 2–77, a wall in the link has been moved but the monitored wall in the host file has not been moved. How do you align the wall in the host file with the wall in the linked file? (Select all that apply.)

RVT Links : Linked Revit Model : Warehouse.rvt : 2 : location <Not Shared>

Figure 2–77

a. Move the wall in the host file so it matches the location in the linked file.

b. Run Coordination Review and select **Accept the difference**.

c. Run Coordination Review and select **Modify Wall**.

d. Run Interference Check and select **Match Centerlines**.

Command Summary

Button	Command	Location
	Bind Link (convert link to group)	• **Ribbon**: *Modify	RVT Links* tab>Link panel
	Copy/Monitor	• **Ribbon**: *Collaborate* tab>Coordinate panel
	Coordination Review	• **Ribbon**: *Collaborate* tab>Coordinate panel
	Interference Check	• **Ribbon**: *Collaborate* tab>Coordinate panel
	Link (convert group to link)	• **Ribbon**: *Modify	Model Groups* tab>Group panel • **Shortcut: LG (when a group is selected)**
	Link Revit	• **Ribbon**: *Insert* tab>Link panel
	Manage Links	• **Ribbon**: *Insert* tab>Link panel or *Modify RVT Links* tab>Link panel (if selected)
	Reconcile Hosting	• **Ribbon**: *Collaborate* tab>Coordinate panel

Chapter 3

Importing and Exporting

Files from CAD programs can be linked and imported into a Revit® project, then the elements within the CAD files can be traced over or used as is to create a hybrid project. Imported CAD files can be manipulated and even exploded into individual elements, which can then take on Revit properties. Raster images and PDF files can also be linked or imported into a Revit project. Information stored in Revit files can also be exported for use in CAD programs. The detailed building information that is stored in a project can be exported to other file formats that include DWF, DGN, and IFC. Further, information that is exported to a gbXML file can be used in energy analysis programs.

Learning Objectives

- Import or link files that were created in other CAD programs into a Revit project.
- Query elements and delete layers in imported/linked CAD files.
- Explode imported CAD files.
- Import/link and modify raster images.
- Import/link PDF files.
- Export Revit projects to other file formats, including CAD formats and DWF files.
- Export information contained in a project to gbXML that can be used in other energy analysis software.

3.1 Importing and Linking CAD Files

Many firms have legacy drawings from CAD programs or could be working with consultants that use them. For example, you may want to link an AutoCAD DWG plan into your project, as shown in the Link CAD Formats dialog box in Figure 3–1, that you would then trace over using Revit tools. Other non-CAD specific file formats, including coordination models from Navisworks, IFC files and point clouds, can also be opened or linked into Revit projects.

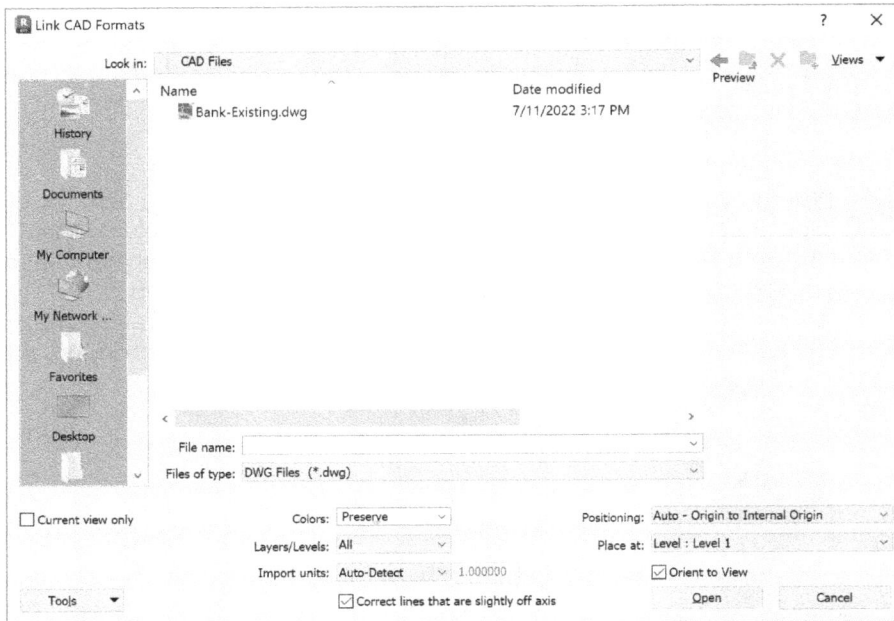

Figure 3–1

CAD file formats that can be imported or linked include AutoCAD$^{\circledR}$ (DWG and DXF), MicroStation (DGN), 3D ACIS modeling kernel (SAT), Trimble SketchUp (SKP), FormIt (AXM), 3D Shape (OBJ and STL), and Rhino (3dm).

> *Note: You can print a hybrid drawing – part Revit project and part imported/linked drawing.*

Linking vs. Importing

- **Link:** A connection is maintained with the original file and the link updates if the original file is updated.
- **Import:** No connection is maintained with the original file. It becomes a separate element in the Revit model.

How To: Link or Import a CAD File

1. The dialog boxes for Link CAD and Import CAD formats are the same except for the positioning method. Proceed as follows:

To...	Then...
Link a CAD file	In the *Insert* tab>Link panel, click ⬚ (Link CAD).
Import a CAD file	In the *Insert* tab>Import panel, click ⬚ (Import CAD).

2. Fill out the Link CAD (or Import CAD) dialog box. The top part of the dialog box holds the standard select file options.

3. Expand the Files of type drop-down list to specify the file type you want to link or import into your Revit project, as shown in Figure 3–2.

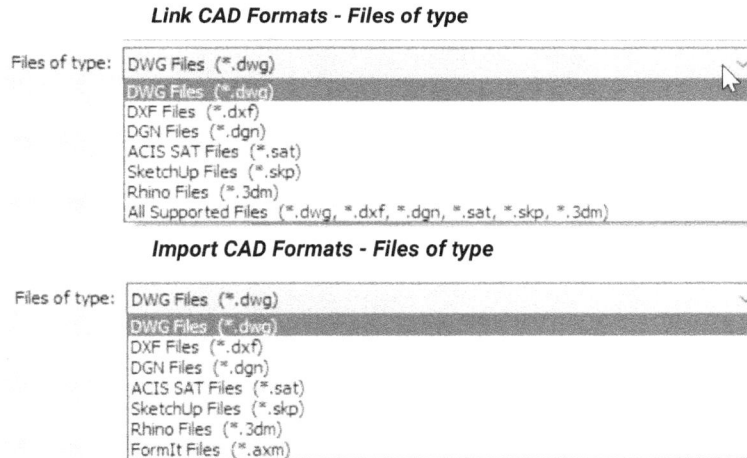

Link CAD Formats - Files of type

Import CAD Formats - Files of type

Figure 3–2

4. Continue to fill out the dialog box. The bottom outlines the various options for linking or importing, as shown in Figure 3–3.

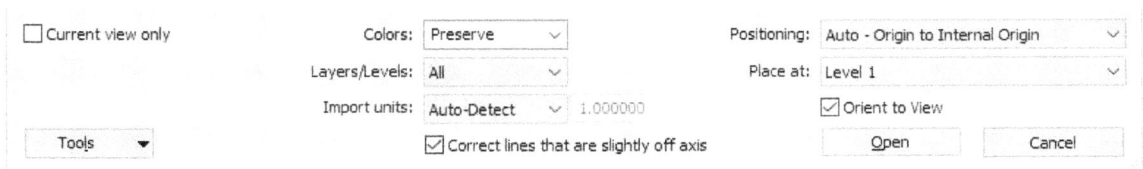

Figure 3–3

5. Click **Open**.

- Depending on the selected positioning method, the file is automatically placed or you can place it with the cursor.

Link and Import Options

Current view only	If selected, the file is imported/linked into the current view and not into other views. You might want to enable this option if you are just working on a floor plan and do not want the objects to display in 3D and other views.
Colors	Revit works mainly with black lines of different weights on a white background to describe elements, but both AutoCAD and MicroStation use a variety of colors. To make the move into Revit easier, you can select to turn all colors to Black and White, Preserve colors, or Invert colors
Layers	You can select which layers from the original drawing are imported/linked. The options are All, Visible (those that are not off or frozen), and Select. Select opens a list of layers or levels from which you can select when you import the drawing file.
Import units	Revit can auto-detect the units in the imported/linked file. You can also specify the units that you want to use from a list of typical Imperial and Metric units or set a Custom scale factor.
Correct lines that are slightly off axis	Corrects lines that are less than 0.1 degree of axis so that any elements based on those line are created correctly. It is on by default. Toggle it off if you are working with site plans.
Positioning	Select from the methods to place the imported/linked file in the Revit host project. If linking the file, Auto - By Shared Coordinates is available.

Place at:	Select a level in the drop-down list to specify the vertical positioning for the file. This is grayed out if you have selected Current view only.
	When linking or importing a CAD file, you can specify a level or a named horizontal reference plane in the project to position the CAD file at.
Orient to View	Select this to place the file at the same orientation as the current view.

- The default positioning is **Auto - Origin to Internal Origin**. The software remembers the most recently used positioning type as long as you are in the same session of Revit. (The CAD Links dialog box remembers the last positioning used separately from the RVT Links dialog box.)

- If you are linking a file, an additional positioning option, **Auto-By Shared Coordinates**, is available. It is typically used with linked Revit files. If you use it with a CAD file, an alert box opens, as shown in Figure 3–4, containing information about the coordinate systems and what Revit does.

Differing Coordinate Systems   ✕

The host model and the link do not share the same coordinate system. The link's World coordinates will be aligned with this project's Shared coordinates.

Close

Figure 3–4

- When you link a DWG file that includes reference files (XREFs), as shown in AutoCAD's External References palette in Figure 3–5, only files whose *Type* is set to **Attach** will display. Files whose *Type* is set to **Overlay** do not display. Also, if the reference files are unloaded, they will not display.

Figure 3–5

- When you import a DWG file, all XREFs display no matter how they are set up in the DWG file.

Importing Line Weights

One significant setting for imported drawings is the line weight. Both AutoCAD and MicroStation can use line weights as well as colors. Typically, AutoCAD line weights are associated with a color; therefore, Revit imports them by color.

How To: Import Line Weights

1. Before you import a CAD file, in the *Insert* tab>Import panel, click ⌐ (Import Line Weights), as shown in Figure 3–6.

Import Line Weights

Maps pen numbers from layers of a DWG or DXF file to Revit line weights.

When you import a DWG or DXF file, each layer in the file is assigned a line weight based on the pen number-line weight settings. The software can import pen numbers from an imported file and map them to a Revit line weight. You can then save these mappings in a text file.

Press F1 for more help

Figure 3–6

Note: Clicking ⌐ in the title bar of a panel typically opens a settings dialog box related to the commands in the panel.

2. In the Import Line Weights dialog box, shown in Figure 3–7, load a text file that holds the relationships or type them in the dialog box. You can then save them for later use.

Figure 3-7

3. Click **OK** and then import the CAD file.

• To load information from an existing text file, click **Load...** and select the file that you want to use. Several files are included in the *Data* folder, as shown in Figure 3-8.

Figure 3-8

• To create a custom text file for specific projects, set up a sequence and click **Save As...**.

• Save your custom import line weight text files to a folder that is accessible to everyone that might need to use it. Do not save any custom files to default Revit folders because they might be deleted if the program is upgraded or reinstalled.

> **Hint: Linking Autodesk Civil 3D DWG Files**
>
> Autodesk Civil 3D creates DWG files but the process of using them accurately in Revit requires some extra steps. The Project Base Point in Revit is basically the same as the 0,0,0 origin point in an AutoCAD DWG. However, Civil 3D files typically use real-world site locations established by surveyors. You can request a reference point (Northing, Easting, Elevation) from the civil engineer and add that information to the Survey Point in the Revit project before linking the site into the model.

Working with Other File Formats

There are additional file formats that can be opened or linked into Revit projects, including IFC (Industry Foundation Class) elements, point clouds and coordination models. ADSK (Autodesk Exchange) files can be loaded and used as a family.

IFC (Industry Foundation Classes)

The IFC specification is an international data neutral format. Models created in any building design program can be saved or exported to this file format. You can open IFC files directly (*File* tab>Open> (IFC)) or link them into the current project (in the *Insert* tab>Link panel, click (Link IFC)).

- If you are opening an IFC file, first set up the default template and manage the mapping of IFC classes to Revit Categories (*File* tab>Open> (IFC Options)).
- Revit models can be exported to IFC.

Point Clouds

Point clouds are created using 3D laser scanners and are frequently used to establish accurate existing information. Once you link a point cloud (in the *Insert* tab>Link panel click (Point Cloud)) into a project, as shown in Figure 3–9, you can snap to alignment planes and individual points.

Figure 3–9

There are two file formats that you can link:

- • **RCS:** Individual indexed scanned models.
- • **RCP:** Groups of indexed scanned models.

- Raw format point clouds must first be converted to RCS or RCP files using Autodesk®
  Recap® before being imported into Revit.

How To: Link a Point Cloud

1. In the *Insert* tab>Link panel, click (Point Cloud).

2. In the Link Point Cloud dialog box, specify the *Positioning* (Auto - Center to Center, Auto -
   Origin to Internal Origin, or Auto - By Shared Coordinates), as shown in Figure 3–10, and
   click **Add...**.

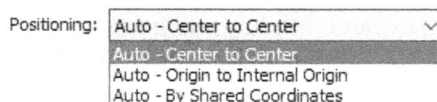

Figure 3–10

- In the Visibility/Graphic Overrides dialog box, in the P*oint Clouds* tab, you can change the
  visibility and set a color mode. Each individual scan can be controlled individually.

Coordination Models

Many construction projects include designs from a variety of Autodesk software programs. Autodesk® Navisworks® enables you to link together files from these different programs to create a coordination model. You can then link the models saved in Navisworks as a NWD or NWC file into your Revit model, to help you coordinate the larger project, as shown in Figure 3–11.

Figure 3–11

How To: Link a Coordination Model

1. In the *Insert* tab>Link panel, expand (Coordination Model) and select (Local).
2. In the Select File dialog box, navigate to the Navisworks model (.NWD or .NWC), set the *Positioning*, and click **Open**.

3.2 Modifying Imported Files

When you select an imported/linked file, you can modify it by arranging the Foreground/ Background status, modifying its Type Properties, querying information about elements in the file, and deleting layers. You can also modify the Visibility/Graphic Overrides of each imported/ linked instance.

*   An imported/linked file is called an Import Symbol once it is inserted into a project, as shown in Figure 3-12.

Figure 3-12

Arranging Imported Files

When you import/link a CAD file into the current view, it is view-specific and you can arrange it with respect to the model elements in the project. To do this, in the Options Bar or in Properties, change the *Draw Layer* to either **Background** or **Foreground**, as shown in Figure 3-13.
Important: These options display if the imported/linked instance was imported by **Current view only** or into a drafting view.

Figure 3-13

- If a file is linked/imported with **Current view only** selected, you can also move imported/linked files incrementally using **Bring to Front** and **Send to Back** in the Arrange panel, as shown in Figure 3–14.

Figure 3–14

Modifying Type Properties

The *Instance Scale* and the *Name* of the file are Type Properties. Select the import/linked

instance you want to modify and click (Edit Type) to open the Type Properties dialog box, as shown in Figure 3–15.

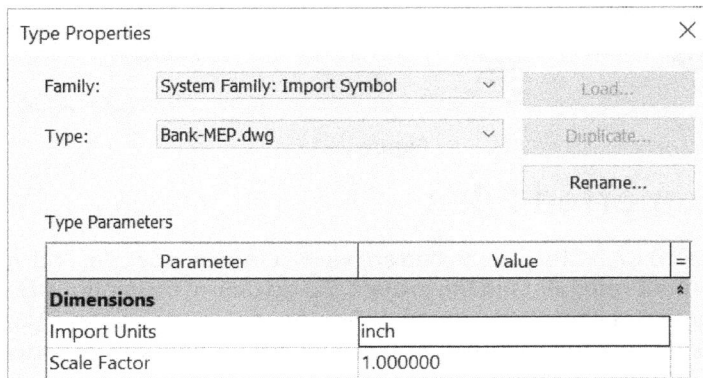

Figure 3–15

- If you change the *Import Units*, the *Scale Factor* is automatically updated. If the *Import Units* are the same type as the host units, you can change the *Scale Factor* independently. You might need to do this if the original file was scanned and not necessarily accurately to scale.

- You can also change the scale using (Scale). This command is not typically used on other Revit elements.

- Imported/linked instances can be part of a group. If they are placed in the current view, they are the only ones to be considered detail elements, otherwise they will be considered model elements.

Querying Imported Files

When working with imported/linked files, it often helps to know what type of objects you are dealing with, without having to modify the file in any way. The **Query** command gives you this information and also enables you to delete or hide the layer of the selected object.

How To: Query Imported/Linked Files

1. Select the imported/linked file that you want to query.

2. In the *Modify* contextual tab>Import Instance panel, click ⊕ (Query).

3. Select the element in the imported/linked file about which you want to inquire. The Import Instance Query dialog box displays information about the objects, as shown in Figure 3–16.

Figure 3–16

- Click **OK** if you just want to look at the object's information.
- Click **Delete** to remove all objects on the layer referenced by the selected object.
- Click **Hide in View** to hide (but not delete) all objects on the layer referenced by the selected object.

4. You are still in the **Query** command and can select other items in the file.

5. Press <Esc> to end the command.

Deleting Layers

If you are creating a hybrid file and there are layers or levels in the imported/linked file that you do not need in the project, you can delete them without exploding the imported file.

- Only items on the selected layers are removed. What is actually on those layers depends on how well the original drafters followed the layering guidelines.

- If deleting layers from a linked file, the layers and items on them are deleted inside the Revit project only. The original file is not changed.

How To: Delete Layers in Imported/Linked Files

1. Select the imported/linked file.

2. In the *Modify* contextual tab>Import Instance panel, click (Delete Layers).

3. The Select Layers/Levels to Delete dialog box displays a list of all layers or levels in the drawing, as shown in Figure 3−17.

Figure 3−17

4. Select the layers or levels that you want to delete from the imported/linked file and click **OK**.

Hint: Exploding Imported Files

Exploding CAD files is a dangerous action and is not recommended in most situations as it increases the file size of the project and leaves behind a variety of undesirable 2D elements. However, if this action is absolutely necessary, there are several commands to help. Select the imported file and in the *Modify* contextual tab>Import Instance panel, expand **Explode**

and click (Full Explode) or (Partial Explode).

- Full Explode converts everything to Revit objects.
- Partial Explode converts all top-level objects but does not explode reference files or blocks in the imported drawing, as shown in Figure 3–18.

Figure 3–18

- Linked files cannot be exploded.

Modifying the Visibility of Imported Files

If you have used the imported/linked file as a guideline for tracing, you can toggle off the visibility of the entire image without removing it from the project in case you need it later. You can also toggle off individual layers or levels.

How To: Hide Individual Layers

1. Open the Visibility/Graphic Overrides dialog box.

2. Switch to the *Imported Categories* tab. It displays a list for each imported instance, as well as its layers/levels, as shown in Figure 3–19.

3. To have the linked/imported file display in halftone, check the box in the **Halftone** column.

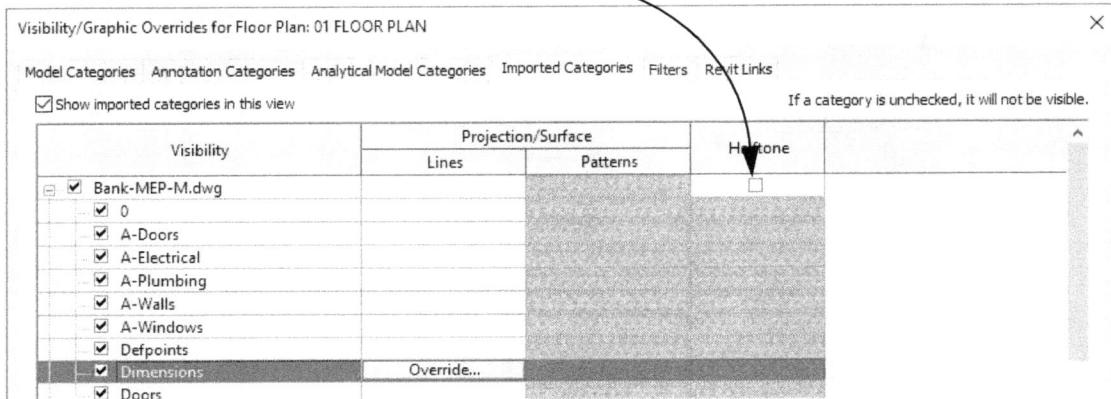

Figure 3–19

4. Click the plus sign beside the file name to expand a list of the layers or levels in that file.

5. Clear the checkmark from the individual layers that you do not want to display.

   - Typically, these layers contain similar information, such as all windows or all notes in a drawing. However, it is not as definite as using Revit elements. An item might have been misplaced on a different layer and if so, it does not toggle off.

6. Close the dialog box.

- To toggle off the entire file, clear the checkmark next to the file name.

Temporarily Hide/Isolate

You might want to temporarily remove linked or imported files from a view, modify the project, and then restore the elements. Instead of completely toggling the elements off, you can temporarily hide them.

Select the elements you want to hide (make invisible) or isolate (keep displayed while all other elements are hidden) and click ⌀ (Temporary Hide/Isolate). Select the method you want to use, as shown in Figure 3–20.

Figure 3–20

- The category or elements are hidden or isolated. A cyan border displays around the view with a note in the upper left corner, as shown in Figure 3–21. It indicates that the view contains temporarily hidden or isolated elements.

Temporary Hide/Isolate

Figure 3–21

- Click ⚭ (Temporary Hide/Isolate) again and select **Reset Temporary Hide/Isolate** to restore the elements to the view.

- If you want to permanently hide the elements in the view, select **Apply Hide/Isolate to View**.

- Elements that are temporarily hidden in a view are not hidden when the view is printed.

Hide Graphics in a View

When working in views, you can quickly hide the linked or imported file by selecting it and typing **VH**. To hide the imported or linked file, select it and right-click to display the shortcut menu, then select **Hide in View** and select either **Elements** or **Category**, as shown in Figure 3–22. These options are also available in the contextual ribbon, as shown in Figure 3–23.

Figure 3–22

Figure 3–23

Practice 3a
Link a CAD File - Architectural

Practice Objectives

- Link an AutoCAD file into a Revit project and use it as a basis to add elements for a hybrid drawing.
- Query elements in the linked file and delete extraneous layers.

In this practice, you will create a hybrid CAD/Revit project for an addition to an existing building. You will link an AutoCAD file into a project and add some Revit elements, as shown in Figure 3–24. You will then query elements in the linked file, toggle off layers, and delete layers from the project.

Figure 3–24

Task 1: Link a CAD file and add Revit elements.

1. Start a new project based on the Metric-architectural template found in the practice files *Templates* folder.

2. Save the project as **Arch-Bank-Addition-M.rvt** in your practice files *Architectural* folder.

3. Verify that you are in the **Floor Plans: Level 1** view.

4. In the *Insert* tab>Link panel, click 🔲 (Link CAD).

5. In the Link CAD dialog box, in the practice files *Architectural>CAD Files* folder, select the AutoCAD drawing file **Bank-Existing-M.dwg** and set the following options:

   - Select **Current view only**
   - *Colors:* **Black and White**
   - *Layers:* **All**
   - *Import Units:* **Auto-Detect**
   - Select **Correct lines that are slightly off axis**
   - *Positioning:* **Auto - Center to Center**

6. Click **Open**.

7. Open the Visibility/Graphic Overrides dialog box and select the *Imported Categories* tab.

8. Check the box in the *Halftone* column for **Bank-Existing-M.dwg**, as shown in Figure 3–25

Figure 3–25

9. Click **OK**.

10. Switch to an elevation view. No elements are in that view because the imported information was from a linked file that was linked in **Floor Plans: Level 1** with **Current view only** selected.

    *Note: If this DWG was linked with **Current view only** unchecked, there would only be a solid line in the elevation view because the DWG is 2D only.*

11. Switch to **Floor Plans: Level 2**. You will not see the linked file because it was linked in **Floor Plans: Level 1** with **Current view only** selected.

12. Switch back to the **Floor Plans: Level 1** view.

13. Use the outline in front of the lobby and vestibule to draw exterior **Generic - 300mm** walls (with the *Height* set to **Level 2**). Add doors (you will need to load a double door from the practice files *Architectural>Families* folder) and windows in front of the existing entrance of the building as a new entrance, similar to that shown in Figure 3–26.

Figure 3–26

14. Switch to the **Elevations (Building Elevations): South** view. You should see the Revit objects in the view.

15. Save the project.

Task 2: Query and modify the visibility of elements in the linked CAD file.

1. Return to the **Floor Plans: Level 1** view.

2. Select the linked CAD file. In the *Modify | Bank-Existing-**M**.dwg* tab>Import Instance panel, click (Query).

3. Select the toilet bowl in the Toilet room. It is a block from AutoCAD on the layer **Plumbing**, as shown in Figure 3–27.

Figure 3–27

4. Click **Hide in View**. This and the other block are removed from the view.

5. Click **Modify** or press <Esc> to end the query, then zoom out to see the entire building.

6. Open the Visibility/Graphic Overrides dialog box. Switch to the *Imported Categories* tab.

7. Click the node ("+") next to **Bank-Existing-M.dwg** to expand the layers. Toggle off the **Text** and **Furniture** layers. Click **OK**.

8. The cabinetwork of the tellers' booths is toggled off but the text still displays, as shown in Figure 3–28. Note that the text that was supposed to be on this layer, is actually on a different layer.

Figure 3–28

9. Select the linked CAD file, use ![Query icon] (Query) to select the text, and click **Hide in view** to hide it in the view.

10. Click **Modify**.

11. Elements on several layers are not required for this project. Select the linked CAD file in the project. In the *Modify | Bank-Existing-M.dwg* tab>Import Instance panel, click ![Delete Layers icon] (Delete Layers).

12. Select the layers **Header**, **Furniture**, and **Plumbing** in the Select Layers/Levels to Delete dialog box, as shown in Figure 3–29, and click **OK**.

Figure 3–29

13. Save and close the project.

End of practice

Practice 3b
Link a CAD File - Structural

Practice Objectives

- Link an AutoCAD file into a Revit project and use it as a basis to add elements for a hybrid drawing.
- Query elements in the imported file and delete extraneous layers.

In this practice, you will create a hybrid CAD/Revit project for an addition to an existing building. You will link an AutoCAD file into a project and add some Revit elements, as shown in Figure 3-30. You will then query elements in the linked file, toggle off layers, and delete layers from the project.

New Revit elements

Figure 3-30

Task 1: Link a CAD file.

1. Start a new project based on the Metric Structural Template found in the practice files *Templates* folder.
2. Save the project as **Struct-Bank-Addition-M.rvt** in your practice files *Structural* folder.
3. Verify that you are in the **Structural Plans: Level 2** view.

4. In the *Insert* tab>Link panel, click ⌑ (Link CAD).

5. In the Import CAD dialog box, in the practice files *Structural>CAD Files* folder, select the AutoCAD drawing file **Bank-Existing-M.dwg** and set the following options:

   - Select **Current view only**
   - *Colors*: **Black and White**
   - *Layers:* **All**
   - *Import Units:* **Auto-Detect**
   - Select **Correct lines that are slightly off axis**
   - *Positioning*: **Auto - Center to Center**

6. Click **Open**.

7. Open the Visibility/Graphic Overrides dialog box and select the *Imported Categories* tab.

8. Check the box in the *Halftone* column for **Bank-Existing-M.dwg**, as shown in Figure 3–31.

Figure 3–31

9. Click **OK**.

10. Switch to an elevation view. No elements are in that view because the imported information was from a linked file that was linked in **Floor Plans: Level 1** with **Current view only** selected.

    *Note: If this DWG was linked with **Current view only** unchecked, there would only be a solid line in the elevation view because the DWG is 2D only.*

11. Switch to **Structural Plans: Level 1**. You will not see the linked file because it was linked in **Structural Plans: Level 2** with **Current view only** selected.

12. Switch back to the **Structural Plans: Level 2** view.

13. Add structural columns (with a *Depth* set to **Level 1**) and beams to the top of them using the outline in front of the vestibule and lobbies for a new entrance, similar to that shown in Figure 3–32.

Figure 3–32

14. Switch to the **Elevations (Building Elevations): South** view. You should see the Revit objects in the view.

15. Save the project.

Task 2: Query and modify the visibility of elements in the linked CAD file.

1. Return to the **Structural Plans: Level 2** view.

2. Select the linked CAD file. In the *Modify | Bank-Existing-**M**.dwg* tab>Import Instance panel, click ⛭ (Query).

3. Select the toilet bowl in the Toilet room. It is a block from AutoCAD on the layer **Plumbing**, as shown in Figure 3–33.

Figure 3–33

4. Click **Hide in View**. This and the other block are removed from the view.

5. Click **Modify** or press <Esc> to end the query, then zoom out to see the entire building.

6. Open the Visibility/Graphic Overrides dialog box. Switch to the *Imported Categories* tab.

7. Click the "+" next to **Bank-Existing-M.dwg** to expand the layers. Toggle off the **Text** and **Furniture** layers. Click **OK**.

8. The cabinetwork of the tellers' booths is toggled off but the text still displays, as shown in Figure 3–34. Note that the text that was supposed to be on this layer is actually on a different layer.

Figure 3–34

9. Select the linked CAD file, use (Query) to select the text, and click **Hide in view** to hide it in the view.

10. Click **Modify**.

11. Elements on several layers are not required for this project. Select the linked CAD file in the project. In the *Modify | Bank-Existing-M.dwg* tab>Import Instance panel, click (Delete Layers).

12. Select the layers **Header**, **Furniture**, and **Plumbing** in the dialog box, as shown in Figure 3–35, and click **OK**.

Figure 3–35

13. Save and close the project.

End of practice

Practice 3c
Link a CAD File - MEP

Practice Objectives

- Link an AutoCAD file into a Revit project and use it as a basis to add elements for a hybrid drawing.
- Query elements in the imported file and delete extraneous layers.

In this practice, you will create a hybrid CAD/Revit project for an addition to an existing building. You will link an AutoCAD file and a Revit model into a project and add some Revit elements, as shown in Figure 3–36. You will then query elements in an linked CAD file, toggle off layers, and delete layers from the file.

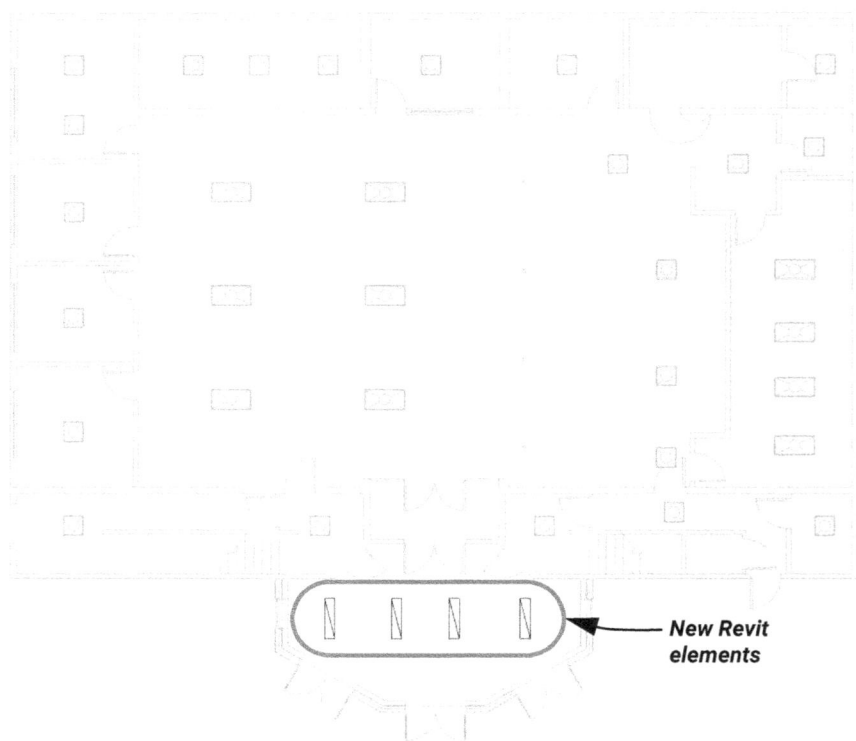

New Revit elements

Figure 3–36

Task 1: Link a CAD file.

1. Start a new project based on the Metric System Template found in the practice files *Templates* folder.

2. Save the project as **Mech-Bank-Addition-M.rvt** in your practice files *MEP* folder.

3. Open the Electrical>Lighting>**Floor Plans: 1- Lighting** view.

4. In the *Insert* tab>Link panel, click 🗋 (Link CAD).

5. In the Link CAD dialog box, in the practice files *MEP>CAD Files* folder, select the AutoCAD drawing file **Bank-MEP-M.dwg**, and set the following options:

    * Select **Current view only**
    * *Colors*: **Black and White**
    * *Layers:* **All**
    * *Import Units:* **Auto-Detect**
    * Select **Correct lines that are slightly off axis**
    * *Positioning*: **Auto - Center to Center**

6. Click **Open**.

7. Open the Visibility/Graphic Overrides dialog box and select the *Imported Categories* tab.

8. Check the box in the *Halftone* column for **Bank-MEP-M.dwg**, as shown in Figure 3–37.

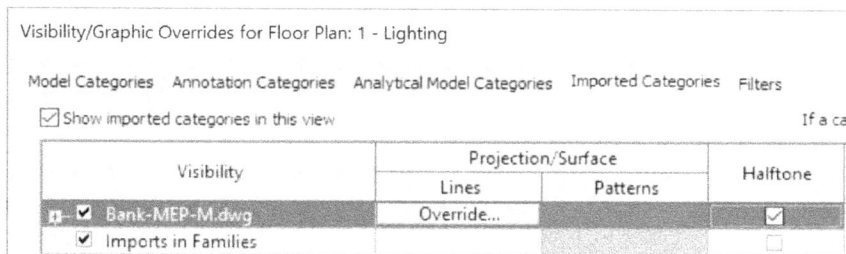

Figure 3–37

9. Click **OK**.

10. Switch to an elevation view. No elements are in that view because the imported information was from a linked file that was linked in **Floor Plans: Level 1** with **Current view only** selected.

    *Note: If this DWG was linked with **Current view only** unchecked, there would only be a solid line in the elevation view because the DWG is 2D only.*

11. Switch to **Floor Plans: 2 - Lighting**. You will not see the linked file because it was linked in **Floor Plans: 1 - Lighting** with **Current view only** selected.

12. Switch back to the **Floor Plans: 1 - Lighting** view.

13. Link in the Revit model **Bank Addition-M.rvt** from your practice files *MEP>Links* folder using **Auto - Internal Origin to Internal Origin** positioning.

14. Open the Electrical>Lighting>Ceiling Plans>**1 - Ceiling Elec** view. The linked Revit elements display in this view but the imported CAD elements do not.

15. Add several new lights in the new entry area similar to that shown in Figure 3–38.

   • If prompted to pick a work plane, select **Pick a Plane** and select the ceiling.

Figure 3–38

16. Switch to the **Elevations (Building Elevations): North-Elec** view. You should see the Revit objects in the view.

17. Save the project.

Task 2: Query and modify the visibility of elements in the linked CAD file.

1. Return to the **Floor Plans: 1 - Lighting** view.

2. Select the linked CAD file. In the *Modify | Bank-MEP-M.dwg* tab>Import Instance panel, click (Query).

3. Select one of the lighting fixtures. It is a block from AutoCAD on the layer **E-LITE-EQPM**, as shown in Figure 3−39. Click **OK**.

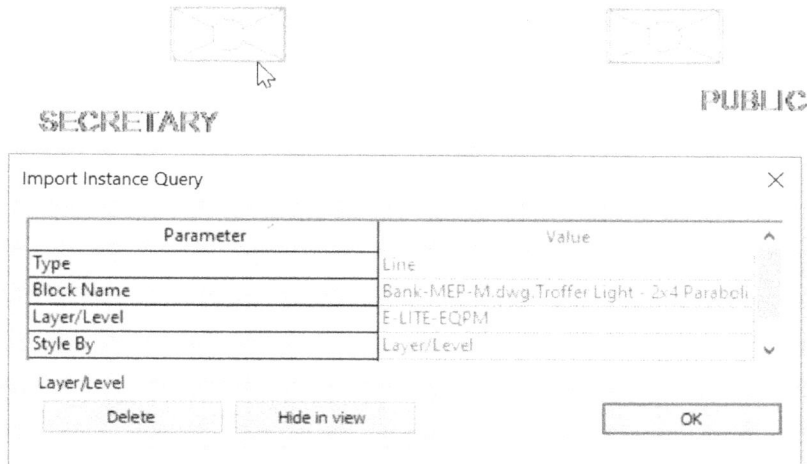

Figure 3−39

4. Select one of the elements in the toilet room. It is a block on layer **Plumbing**. Click **Hide in view**. This and the other block are removed from the view.

5. Click **Modify** or press <Esc> to end the query.

6. Open the Visibility/Graphic Overrides dialog box. Switch to the *Imported Categories* tab.

7. Click the node ("+") next to **Bank-MEP-M.dwg** to expand the layers. Toggle off the **Text** and **Furniture** layers. Click **OK**.

8. The cabinetwork of the tellers' booths is toggled off but the text still displays, as shown in Figure 3–40. Note that the text that was supposed to be on this layer, is actually on a different layer.

Figure 3–40

9. Select the linked CAD file, use (Query) to select the text, and click **Hide in view** to hide it in the view.

10. Click **Modify**.

11. Elements on several layers are not required for this project. Select the linked CAD file in the project. In the Import Instance panel, click (Delete Layers).

12. Select the layers **Furniture** and **Plumbing** in the dialog box, as shown in Figure 3–41, and click **OK**.

Figure 3–41

13. Save and close the project.

End of practice

3.3 Importing and Linking Raster Image and PDF Files

Raster images are made up of pixels, which are essentially dots in a file that create a picture. For example, a raster file is created when you scan a blueprint or other type of drawing, then import or link it into Revit to reference or trace. Another type of raster file is a PDF. Frequently used with text files, programs like Revit and AutoCAD can also create PDF files that can be imported and linked into Revit, as shown in Figure 3–42.

Figure 3–42

- Link a PDF or raster image into a 2D view if you need to reference a file that will be updated throughout the project cycle and to keep the project's file size from increasing when importing files.

- Linked PDFs or raster images can be scaled, rotated, and moved just like an imported PDF or raster image. Any changes made to the PDF or raster image will update when you open your project that it is linked into.

- You cannot link PDFs or raster images while modifying or creating a family in the Family Editor.

Importing/Linking Raster Image Files

A logo used in a title block is often a raster image made in a graphics program, as shown in Figure 3–43. You can add raster images to any 2D view, including sheet files. They can be used as a background view or as part of the final drawing. Imported or linked images are placed behind model objects and annotations.

Figure 3–43

How To: Import and Link a Raster Image

To...	Then...
Import an image file	In the *Insert* tab>Import panel, click 📷 (Import Image).
Link an image file	In the *Insert* tab>Link panel, click 📷 (Link Image).

1. In the Import Image or Link Image dialog box, select the image you want to insert. You can insert .BMP, .JPG, .JPEG, .PNG, and .TIF files.

2. Click **Open**. Four blue dots and an "x" illustrate the default size of the image file, as shown on the left in Figure 3–44. Click on the screen to place the image. It displays with the shape handles still visible, as shown on the right in Figure 3–44.

Figure 3–44

3. Drag the shape handles to resize the graphic, as needed.

Editing Raster Files

Select an imported/linked image to make changes. Once it is selected, you can resize the image as you did when you first inserted it or in Properties, specify *Width* and *Height* values.

- Select **Lock Proportions** in the Options Bar to ensure that the length and width resize proportionally to each other when you adjust the size of an image.

- Use the standard modification tools to **Move**, **Copy**, **Rotate**, **Mirror**, **Array**, and **Scale** images. Images can also be grouped together into Detail Groups.

- The Foreground/Background status can also be set in the Options Bar and in Properties, as shown in Figure 3–45.

Figure 3–45

- In the *Modify | Raster Images* tab>Arrange panel, use the *Arrange* tools, as shown in Figure 3–46, to move images to the front or back of other images or objects.

- You can snap to edges of images, as shown in Figure 3–47.

Figure 3–46

Figure 3–47

Importing/Linking PDF Files

PDF files are often created for sharing information with people that do not have the original program and when you do not want anyone to change the original information. They can also be used as underlays when the original information includes vector data.

How To: Import and Link a PDF File

To...	Then...
Import a PDF file	In the *Insert* tab>Import panel, click ![icon] (Import PDF).
Link a PDF file	In the *Insert* tab>Link panel, click ![icon] (Link PDF).

1. In the Import PDF or Link PDF dialog box, navigate to the location where the PDF file is stored, select it, and click **Open**.

2. In the Import PDF or Link PDF dialog box (Figure 3–48 shows the Import PDF dialog box), select the page you want to import and click **OK**.

Figure 3–48

- Only one page can be imported/linked at a time, but you can import/link additional pages by repeating the process.

3. In Properties, you can specify the size and scale of the image, as shown in Figure 3–49.

- If the PDF comes from a vector source, you can also choose to enable snaps and trace over the elements in the PDF.
- The Foreground/Background status can also be set in the Options Bar and in Properties.

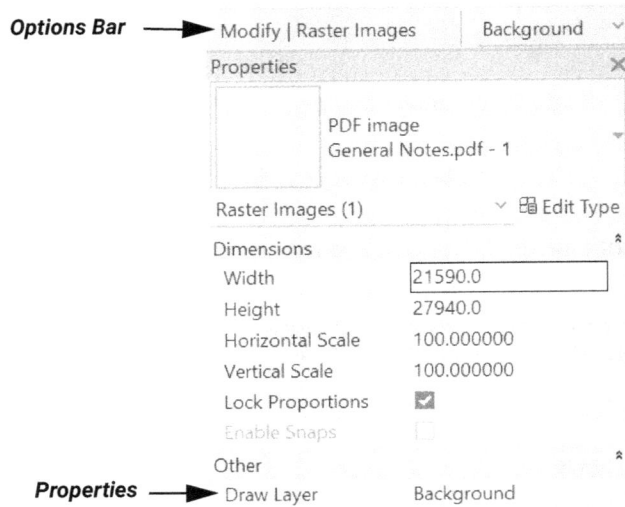

Figure 3–49

Managing Images and PDFs

Both images and PDFs can be modified from within the Manage Links dialog box, from either the *PDF* or *Images* tab.

- You can click **Add...** to add another PDF or image, **Place Instance** to place another instance of the selected PDF or image, or **Show** to open the project view that the PDF or image is in. You can also **Reload From...**, **Reload**, **Unload**, and **Remove** a PDF or image.

- If you have linked a PDF or image, you can change it to be imported instead within the Manage Links dialog box by selecting the link name and clicking the **Import** button.

- Every PDF and image instance is saved. If you delete it in a project view, it will remain in the Manage Links dialog box. You must open the Manage Links dialog box, select the PDF or image, and click **Remove** to delete it from the project.

- You can select more than one instance of PDFs or images within the Manage Links dialog box to reload or remove.

How To: Manage PDFs and Image files

1. In the *Insert* tab>Link panel, click ⌨ (Manage Links), or select the image or PDF and from the *Modify* contextual tab>Image panel, click ⌨ (Manage Links) to open the Manage Links dialog box, as shown in Figure 3–50.

2. Click on the *PDF* or *Images* tab to view the files.

    *   Select a PDF or image to modify or remove it from the project.

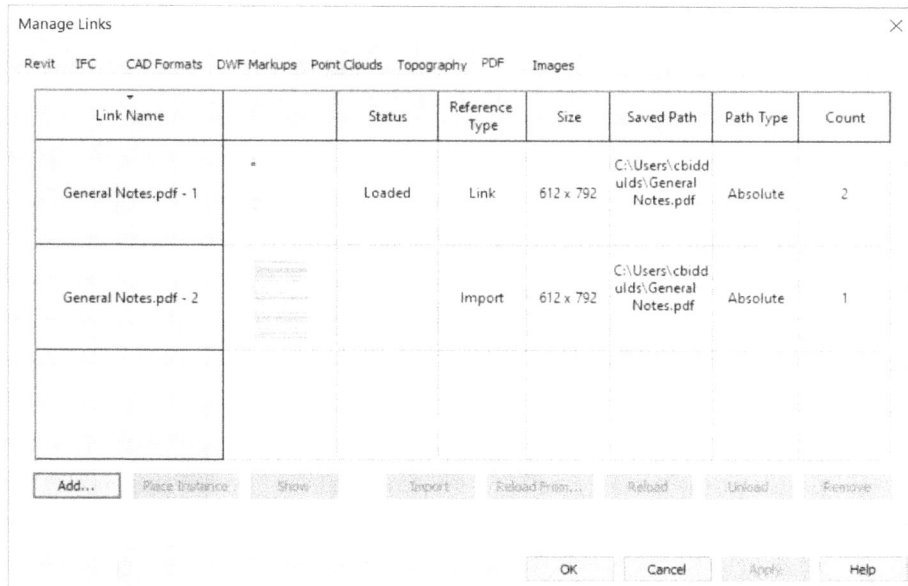

Link Name		Status	Reference Type	Size	Saved Path	Path Type	Count
General Notes.pdf - 1		Loaded	Link	612 x 792	C:\Users\cbidd ulds\General Notes.pdf	Absolute	2
General Notes.pdf - 2			Import	612 x 792	C:\Users\cbidd ulds\General Notes.pdf	Absolute	1

Manage Links

Revit   IFC   CAD Formats   DWF Markups   Point Clouds   Topography   PDF   Images

Add...   Place Instance   Show   Import   Reload From...   Reload   Unload   Remove

OK   Cancel   Apply   Help

Figure 3–50

Practice 3d
Import and Link Image and PDF Files - All Disciplines

Practice Objectives

- Add a rendered raster image to a sheet.
- Add a multi-page PDF to a sheet.

In this practice, you will add a rendered image of a new entrance to a sheet and add a multi-page PDF with General Notes to the same sheet, as shown in Figure 3–51.

Figure 3–51

Task 1: Add a PDF and image to a project file.

1. From the practice files *General* folder, open **Bank-Title-M.rvt**

2. Verify the opened view is **CS 101 - Cover Sheet**.

3. In the *Insert* tab>Link panel, click ![icon] (Link Image). Select the image file **Entrance.jpg** (from your practice files *General>Images* folder) and place it on the sheet.

4. Move and resize it so that it fits on the sheet, as shown in Figure 3–52.

Figure 3–52

5. In the *Insert* tab>Import panel, click 📋 (Import PDF).

6. In the Import PDF dialog box, navigate to the practice files *General>Resources* folder, select **General Notes.pdf**, and click **Open**.

7. In the Import PDF dialog box, select *Page* **1** and click **OK**.

8. Place the text below the image, as shown in Figure 3–53.

Figure 3–53

9. Repeat the process and add page 2 beside page 1.

Task 2: Manage the linked image file.

1. Select the image and from the *Modify | Raster Images* tab> Image panel, select ⌗ (Manage Links).

2. In the Manage Links dialog box, from the *Images* tab, note that the Entrace.jpg's *Reference Type* is **Link**, as shown in Figure 3–54.

Manage Links							✕
Revit IFC CAD Formats DWF Markups Point Clouds Topography PDF Images							

Link Name		Status	Reference Type	Size	Saved Path	Path Type	Count
Entrance.jpg		Loaded	Link	1896 x 884	\Revit Collaboration Tools Practice Files\General\Images\Entrance.jpg	Absolute	1

Figure 3–54

3. Select the image and click the **Import** button at the bottom of the dialog box. The image's *Reference Type* is now set to **Import**.

4. Save and close the project.

End of practice

3.4 Exporting Files

If your company uses multiple CAD programs or works with consultants who use other CAD programs, prepare your Revit files so that the other programs can use them as well. The Revit software provides ways to export Revit data to CAD formats, DWF/DWFx, Images and Animations, Reports, FBX, gbXML, IFC (Industry Foundation Classes), and ODBC databases, as shown in Figure 3–55.

> *Note: Scroll down the Export list to see additional options.*

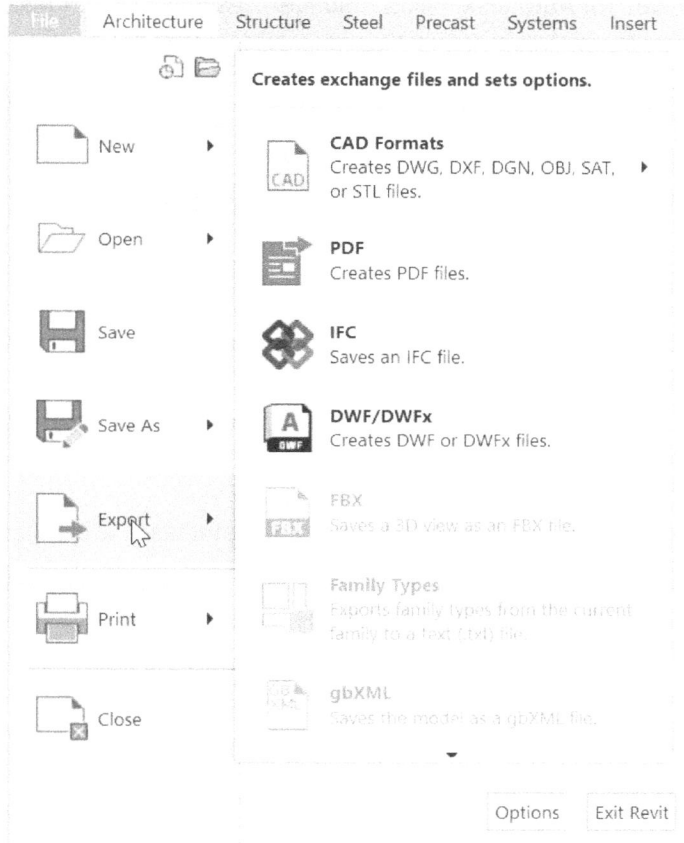

Figure 3–55

- Find out if the users for which you are exporting need a 2D or 3D view. You can export any view, but only 3D views export the entire building model; other views create 2D files.

- Text character size, location, and other text related properties is rendered faithfully when exported to other CAD file formats.

Export Types

- **CAD Formats:** Exports projects to AutoCAD DWG or DXF, MicroStation DGN, or ASIC SAT files for 3D modeling.

- **PDF:** Exports selected views and sheets directly from Revit to a PDF file. This can be a single, multi-page PDF file or several individual PDF files.

- **DWF/DWFx:** Exports views and sheets to DWF or DWFx files to be used in Autodesk® Design Review for review and redlining.

- **FBX:** Exports 3D files for Autodesk® MotionBuilder®, as well as Autodesk® Maya®, Autodesk® 3ds Max®, and Viz plug-ins. You must be in a 3D view for this to display.

- **Family Types:** Exports family type information to a text (.txt) file that can be imported into a spreadsheet program to verify that all of the parameters for each type are correct. You must be in a family file for this to display.

- **gbXML:** Exports model information that can be used in other programs for energy or load analysis.

- **IFC:** Exports the Revit model to Industry Foundation Class objects. These can be used by CAD programs that do not use RVT file formats. It uses established standards for typical objects in the building industry. For example, a Revit wall element translates to an IfcWall object. Additional mapping for specialty items can be set up.

- **ODBC Database:** Exports Revit information to an Open Database Connectivity database file. It creates tables of the model element types and instances, levels, rooms, key schedules, and assembly codes.

- **Images and Animations:** Exports walkthroughs, solar studies, and images.

- **Reports:** Exports information from Schedules and Room/Area. Schedules are exported as delimited text files that can be imported into a spreadsheet. You must be in a schedule view to export. Room/Area reports are saved as HTML files.

- **Options:** Sets up the options for Export Setups for DWG/DXF, DGN, and IFC options.

- **NWC:** (Navisworks NWC Export Utility installs only) If you have the Navisworks NWC Export Utility 2024 installed, you will see the option to export to an NWC file type.

Exporting CAD Format Files

Exporting Revit Projects to various CAD file formats is a common need in collaboration with consultants and engineers. Using this process, you can export individual views or sheets, or sets of views or sheets to DWG, DXF, DGN, and SAT files. You can also create and save sets of views/sheets.

- To improve performance and file size of the exported file, you will want to use Visibility/ Graphic Overrides to turn off objects that are not being seen in the view you are exporting.

- Use a section box or crop region to minimize elements outside the region.

- Reduce the amount of detail by setting the view's detail level to Coarse or Medium.

How To: Export a CAD Format File

1. If you are exporting only one view, open the view you want to export. If you are exporting the model, open a 3D view.

2. In the *File* tab, expand (Export), click (CAD Formats), and select the type of format you want to export, as shown in Figure 3–56.

Figure 3–56

- The examples in this section show the process for DWG files. It is the same for other types of files.

3. The respective dialog box displays, such as the DWG Export dialog box shown in Figure 3–57.

Figure 3–57

4. If you have an existing export setup, you can select it from the drop-down list as shown in Figure 3–58, or click ⎡...⎤ (Modify Export Setup) to create a new one.

Figure 3–58

5. Select the view(s) you want to export from the Export drop-down list as shown in Figure 3–59.

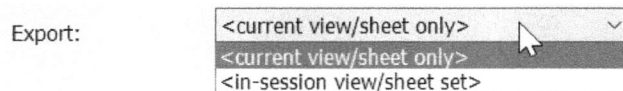

Figure 3–59

* To export only the active view, select **<current view/sheet only>**.

* To export any views or sheets that are open in the session of Revit, select **<in-session view/sheet set>**.

* To export a predefined set of views or sheets, select the name from the list if it is available. You can create new sets of views and sheets to export.

6. When everything is set up correctly, click **Next...**.

7. In the Export CAD Formats - Save to Target Folder dialog box, select the folder location and name. If you are exporting to DWG or DXF, select the version in the Files of type drop-down list.

8. Click **OK**.

• The Project Base Point of the Revit project becomes the 0,0 coordinate point in other CAD formats.

How To: Create an Export Setup

1. In the DWG, DXF, or DGN Export dialog box, next to the Select Export Setup list, click ⎡...⎤ (Modify Export Setup).

   • Alternatively, in the *File* tab, expand ⬚ (Export)>🔧 (Options) and select 🖾 (Export Setups DWG/DXF) or 🖾 (Export Setups DGN).

2. The Modify DWG/DXF or Modify DGN Export Setup dialog box (shown in Figure 3–60) contains all of the elements and types you can export. You can select an existing Layer standard provided with the program or create a new one.

   • In the *Select Export Setup* section, you can create new export setups, as well as duplicate, rename, and delete setups. These export setup settings can be included in a company template.

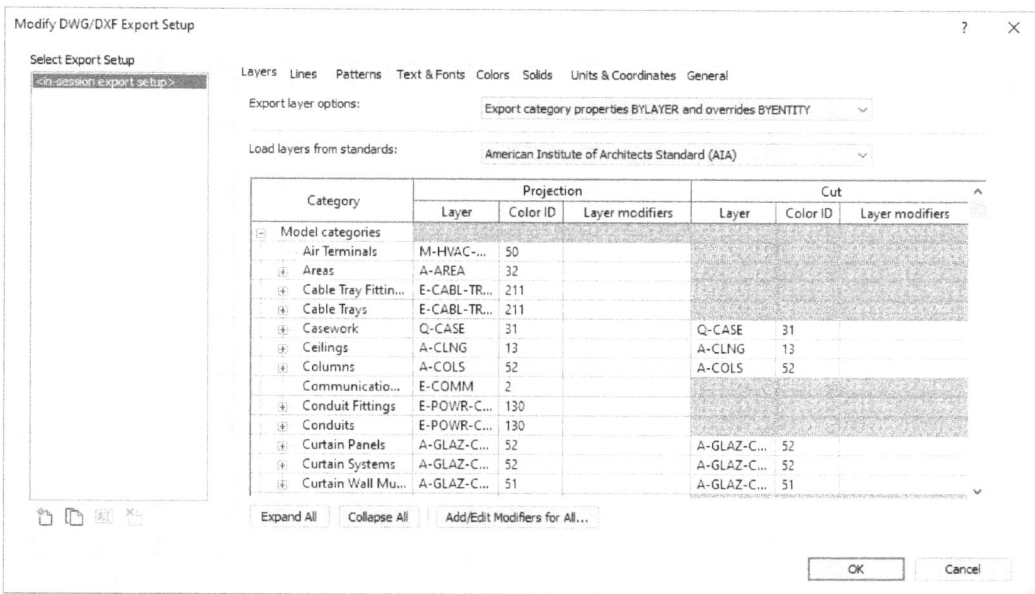

Figure 3–60

3. Select each of the tabs and apply the appropriate information.

- In the *Layers* tab, map the categories in Revit to the layers (or levels).

- In the *Lines*, *Patterns*, and *Text & Fonts* tabs, map the styles required.

- In the *Colors* tab, select to export either Index colors (255 colors) or True color (RGB values).

- In the *Solids* tab (3D views only), select to export to either Polymesh or ACIS solids.

- In the *Units & Coordinates* tab, specify what unit type one DWG unit is and the basis for the coordinate system. In order for the exported Revit file to be in the correct location when XREFed into AutoCAD, you will need to make sure the unit is correct.

  - **Shared Coordinates:** Use this method if you want to maintain the shared coordinates of the Revit host model.

  - **Internal Origin:** Use this method if you have not used shared coordinates in the Revit host model.

  - In the *General* tab, you can set up how the rooms and room boundaries are exported, what to do with any non-plottable layers, how scope boxes, reference planes, coincident lines, and unreferenced view tags are handled, how views on sheets and links are treated, and which version of the DWG file format to use.

- Export setups can be created in a template file or shared between open projects using Transfer Project Standards.

How To: Create a New Set of Views/Sheets to Export

1. Start the appropriate Export CAD Formats command.

2. In the Export CAD Formats dialog box, click ⬜ (New Set).

3. In the New Set dialog box, type a name and click **OK**.

4. The tab displays with the new set active and additional information, as shown in Figure 3–61.

Export:	Plans and Elevations ∨
Show in list:	All views and sheets in the Model ∨

🗂 🗂 AI 🗂   Check All   Check None

Include	Type	Name ▲
☐	🖳	3D View: {3D}
☐	🔼	Elevation: East
☐	🔼	Elevation: North
☐	🔼	Elevation: South
☐	🔼	Elevation: West
☐	🗂	Floor Plan: Site
☐	🗂	Floor Plan: Site Level 1
☐	🗂	Reflected Ceiling Plan: Site ...

Figure 3–61

5. Use *Show in List* to limit the number of items that display in the table.

6. Select the views and/or sheets that you want to export from the project.

   • Use **Check all** or **Check none** to aid in selection.

7. When you finish with the set, continue the export process.

Exporting to DWF

Exporting DWF/DWFx (Design Web Format) files gives you a safe and easy way to share Revit project information without sending the actual file. For example, a client does not have to have Revit on their machine to view the file and they cannot make any changes directly to it. DWF/DWFx files are also much smaller than project files and are therefore easier to email or post on a website. DWF/DWFx files can include element data that can be viewed in Autodesk Design Review.

The process of exporting a DWF file is similar to CAD Format exports. You can export individual views or sheets, as shown in Figure 3–62, or you can create sets of multiple views/sheets by clicking on ▢ (New Set) and selecting from all the views/sheets in the project.

Figure 3–62

- In the *DWF Properties* tab, set up the export object data, the graphics settings, and print setup.

- The *Project Information* tab, shown in Figure 3–63, can be updated and included in a DWF export.

DWF Export Settings		? ✕
Views/Sheets DWF Properties Project Information		

Parameter	Value
Organization Name	
Organization Description	
Building Name	
Author	
Project Issue Date	Issue Date
Project Status	Project Status
Client Name	Owner
Project Address	## Street
Project Name	Project Name
Project Number	Project Number
Route Analysis Settings	Edit...

Figure 3–63

- Files can be exported to the DWF or DWFx format.

- You can mark up (redline) DWF/DWFx files using other programs. The markups can then be linked back into the Revit project, using the 🗋 (DWF Markup) command so the original user can make the changes noted.

- Textures, line patterns, line weights, and text are included in 3D DWF exports.

Export Views and Sheets to PDF

If you do not have a PDF driver to use in the Print dialog box, you can export your views or sheets to PDF.

How To: Export Views and Sheets to PDF

1. In the *File* tab, select ⬚ (Export)>⬚ (PDF).

2. In the PDF Export dialog box (shown in Figure 3–64), enter a file name and the location you would like the PDF to be exported to and set any other settings, as needed.

   - The PDF Export settings are similar to those found in the Revit Print dialog box.

Figure 3–64

3. Click **Export**.

Practice 3e
Export Files - All Disciplines

Practice Objective

* Export views to AutoCAD drawing files and DWF viewing files.

In this practice, you will export several views to AutoCAD drawing files and to DWF files, as shown in Autodesk Design Review in Figure 3–65.

Figure 3–65

Task 1: Set up and export a set of 2D views to a DWG file.

1. In the practice files *General* folder, open **Office-ExportViews-M.rvt**.

2. In the *File* tab, expand [icon] (Export), expand [icon] (CAD Formats), and click [icon] (DWG).

3. In the DWG Export dialog box, in the *Select Export Setup* area, click [icon] (Modify Export Setup).

---

4. In the Modify DWG/DXF Export Setup dialog box, in the *Layers* tab, select the standard you are most likely to use from the *Load layers from standards* list.

5. In the *Text & Fonts* tab, for *Text behavior when exported*, select **Preserve visual fidelity**.

6. Scroll down in the list of fonts and map *Arial* to **Arial Narrow**, as shown in Figure 3–66.

Text Fonts in Revit	Text Fonts in DWG
@Arial Unicode MS	Arial Narrow
@Malgun Gothic	AMGDT_IV25
@Malgun Gothic Semilight	AMGDT_IV50
@Microsoft JhengHei	Arial
@Microsoft JhengHei Light	Arial Black
@Microsoft JhengHei UI	Arial Narrow
	Arial Rounded MT Bold

Layers Lines Patterns Text & Fonts Colors Solids Units & Coordinates General

Text behavior when exported: Preserve visual fidelity

Reset All

Map Revit fonts to fonts in DWG:

Figure 3–66

7. In the *General* tab, select **Export rooms, spaces and areas as polylines**. To create one single export, uncheck **Export views on Sheets and links as external references**.

8. Click **OK**.

9. In the DWG Export dialog box, click ☐ (New Set).

10. In the New Set dialog box, type the name **Plans** and click **OK**.

11. Select at least two floor/structural plan views, as shown in Figure 3–67.

Figure 3–67

12. Click **Next...**.

13. In the Export CAD Formats - Save to Target Folder dialog box, set the *Save In:* to the practice files folder. Set the *Files of Type:* to **AutoCAD 2018 DWG Files (*.dwg)**.

14. Set the *Naming* to **Automatic-Long (Specify prefix)** and type **Plans** in the *File name/prefix* field.

15. Click **OK**. The software generates DWG files for the each selected view using the setup you defined.

Task 2: Export a 3D view to AutoCAD.

1. Switch to a 3D view from the 3D Views section in the Project Browser.

2. In the *File* tab, expand (Export), expand (CAD Formats), and click (DWG).

3. In the DWG Export dialog box, set *Export:* to **<current view/sheet only>**, as shown in Figure 3–68.

Figure 3–68

4. Click **Next....** In the Export CAD Formats - Save to Target Folder dialog box, type a file name, and click **OK**.

5. If you have access to AutoCAD, you can open the files to see the exported geometry or view them in Windows Explorer, as shown in Figure 3–69 in the Extra Large Icons view.

Office-ExportViews-3D View - {3D}.dwg

Office-ExportViews-Floor Plan - 1 - Mech.dwg

Office-ExportViews-Floor Plan - 2 - Mech.dwg

Figure 3–69

Task 3: Export to DWF.

1. In the *File* tab, expand (Export) and click (DWF/DWFx).

2. In the DWF Export Settings dialog box, click (New Set).

3. In the New Set dialog box, type the name **Sheets** and click **OK**.

4. Change the *Show in list:* to **Sheets in the Model** and select the sheets, as shown in Figure 3–70.

Figure 3–70

5. Switch to the *DWF Properties* tab and verify that **Element properties** is selected, as shown in Figure 3–71.

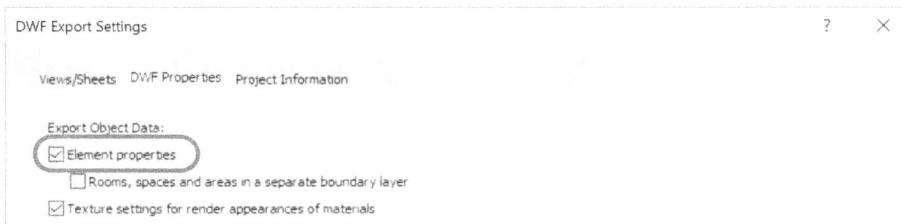

Figure 3–71

6. Click **Next....**

7. In the Export DWF - Save to Target Folder dialog box, in the *File name/prefix* field, add -**Sheets** to the end of the file name, as shown in Figure 3–72. Note that **Combine selected views and sheets into a single dwf file** is selected by default and grayed out because the *Naming*: is set to **Manual (Specify file name)**.

File name/prefix: Office-Export Views-Sheets

Files of type: DWFx Files (*.dwfx)

Naming: Manual (Specify file name)   ☐ Combine selected views and sheets into a single dwf file

OK   Cancel

Figure 3–72

8. Click **OK**.

Note: The Design Review software is a separate download on the Autodesk website.

9. If you have Autodesk Design Review, you can open and view the file.

10. If you do not have the Autodesk Design Review software installed, you can view what the DWF looks like by opening **Office-Export Views-Sheets.DWFx.png**, which can be found in the practice files *General>Images* folder.

11. Save and close all open files.

End of practice

3.5 Exporting for Energy Analysis

Green buildings and energy analysis are now a major component of design. Creating an energy-efficient building requires understanding of how lighting, heating, cooling, and other structures interact with the site, spaces, and materials used. For example, heating and cooling a 3-story space in a cold climate is very different from heating and cooling a room with a low ceiling in a desert area. The seasons and time of day also impact energy consumption, as shown in the shadow study in Figure 3–73.

Figure 3–73

Numerous programs do this type of analysis. Revit projects are Building Information Models (BIM). Therefore, instead of time-consuming hand-takeoff, you can export Revit projects to a gbXML file that can then be imported into the analysis program.

- gbXML stands for <u>G</u>reen <u>B</u>uilding <u>E</u>xtensible <u>M</u>arkup <u>L</u>anguage. It is a standard used to transfer building information from a CAD BIM model to an engineering analysis tool.

- Engineering analysis tools include Green Building Studio, HVAC manufacturer programs (such as Trane or Carrier), and the United States Department of Energy's simulation tool.

- **Subscription-Only Feature:** You can enable the energy model directly in Revit and run energy simulations in the cloud using Autodesk Insight web-based services. This can be done early in a project using either the conceptual mass elements or the building elements without the spaces in place. This does not require exporting to gbXML. The results are hosted in the cloud, and you can compare results from different runs of the program.

Preparing a Project for Energy Analysis

Using the Export to gbXML tool enables you to send information from the energy analytical model based on the energy settings (subscription-only) or the volumes in the model identified by room (architecture) or spaces (MEP).

> *Note: This topic covers exporting using the volumes of rooms and spaces.*

- To prepare a project to export for gbXML you need to verify room height properties and ensure that the volume, as well as the area, is being calculated.

- All interior spaces, including plenums and chases, larger than the Sliver Space Tolerance need to have a room/space element placed in them for accurate analysis.

- For more information on preparing an MEP project for energy analysis, see the ASCENT guide *Autodesk Revit: Fundamentals for MEP*.

How To: Set Up Room Properties for Volumes

1. In the *Architecture* tab>Room & Area panel, click on the title to expand the options, and click ⇨ (Area and Volume Computations).

2. In the Area and Volume Computations dialog box, in the *Computations* tab, select **Areas and Volumes**, as shown in Figure 3–74, so that room volumes are calculated.

Area and Volume Computations

Computations   Area Schemes

  Volume Computations

    Volumes are computed at finish faces.

    ◯ Areas only (faster)

    ⦿ Areas and Volumes

Figure 3–74

3. Click **OK** to close the dialog box.

4. Add rooms to the project that define the spaces and areas for the energy analysis.

5. Modify the room properties so that **Upper Limit** and **Limit Offset** describe the height of the room, as shown in Figure 3–75.

Rooms (1)	⌄ Edit Type
Constraints	≳
Level	Level 1
Upper Limit	Level 1
Limit Offset	4876.8
Base Offset	0.0
Dimensions	≳
Area	38.382 m²
Perimeter	25330.2
Unbounded Height	4876.8
Volume	105.549 m³
Computation Hei...	0.0

Figure 3–75

Exporting to gbXML

When you start the export process, it is recommended that you modify the Project Information and ensure that the spaces and analytical surfaces display as expected. The program calculates the inner room volumes, analytical room models, shading surfaces, openings, and more. An analytical model will be required to export to gbXML.

How To: Export a File to gbXML

1. Apply spaces and zones to the model.
2. In the *Analyze* tab>Energy Optimization panel, click 🌐 (Location).
3. In the Location and Site dialog box, set the location of the project, as shown in Figure 3–76, and click **OK**.

Figure 3–76

4. In the *Analyze* tab>Energy Optimization panel, click 📋 (Energy Settings).

5. In the Energy Settings dialog box (shown in Figure 3–77), review and set settings as needed.

Figure 3–77

6. In the Energy Settings dialog box, in the *Advanced* section, click **Edit...** next to *Other Options*.

7. In the Advanced Energy Settings dialog box, adjust the settings as needed. In the *Room/ Space Data* section, set the *Export Category* to **Spaces**, as shown in Figure 3–78.

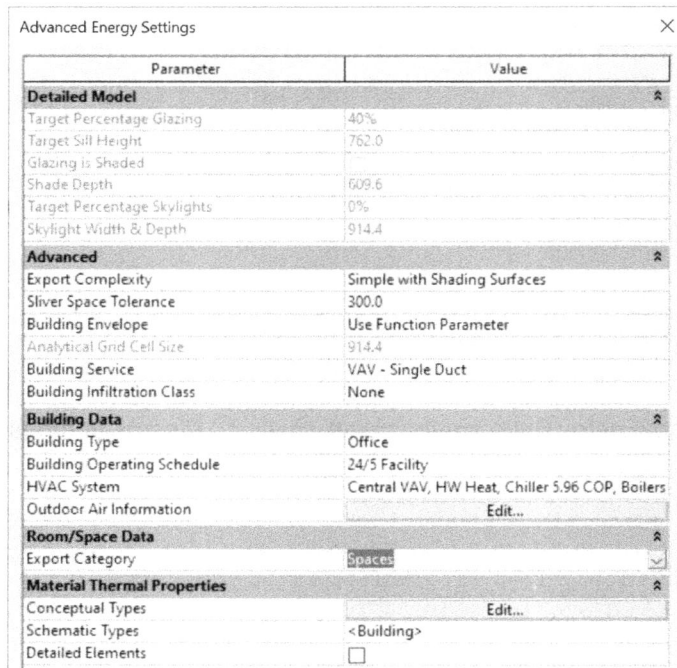

Figure 3–78

8. Click **OK** to close the Advanced Energy Settings dialog box, then click **OK** to close the Energy Settings dialog box.

9. In the *Analyze* tab>Energy Optimization panel, click 🖱 (Create Energy Model). The Create Energy Model dialog box will open notifying you that it may take considerable time to process the model, as shown in Figure 3–79. Click **Create the Energy Analytical Model**.

| Create Energy Model – May Take Considerable Time   ✕ |
| You are about to create the Energy Analytical Model. This may take considerable time during which Revit will not be accessible. What do you want to do? |
| → Create the Energy Analytical Model |
| ☐ Do not show me this message again.   Cancel |
| Click here to learn more |

Figure 3–79

10. Once the model has processed, it will open the **Analytical Spaces** view, as shown in Figure 3–80. The view will also be found in the Project Browser under the Mechanical>???> 3D Views node.

Figure 3–80

- If there are any changes to the spaces, you will need to go to the *Analyze* tab>Energy

  Optimization panel and click (Delete Energy Model), then recreate the energy analytical model.
- Spaces can be reviewed in the System Browser by selecting **Analytical Systems** from the drop-down list, as shown in Figure 3–81.

Figure 3–81

11. To export the Analytical model to gbXML, in the *File* tab, expand (Export) and click (gbXML).

12. In the Create Analytical Spaces dialog box (shown in Figure 3–82), choose the elements/ mode to use for the export.

Figure 3–82

- For more information on which option for elements/mode you should choose, refer to the Help documentation that can be accessed by clicking the **Which elements should I use...** link at the bottom of the dialog box.

13. In the Export gbXML - Save to Target Folder dialog box, select the folder location and name for the file and click **Save**.

Practice 3f
Export for Energy Analysis

Practice Objectives

- Prepare a project for export to gbXML.
- Create the energy analytical model and review analytical spaces.

In this practice, you will prepare a project and run the **Export to gbXML** command. You will then create an analytical model and review the analytical spaces.

Task 1: Prepare the project for gbXML.

1. In the practice files *MEP* folder, open **Mech-Analysis-M.rvt**.

2. In the *Analyze* tab>Energy Optimization panel, click 🌐 (Location).

3. In the Location and Site dialog box, set the *Project Address* to a location of your choice. Note your location will display in the right-hand pane. If the address shown is not the exact location, you can move the red arrow to a precise location, as shown in Figure 3–83. Click **OK** to close the dialog box.

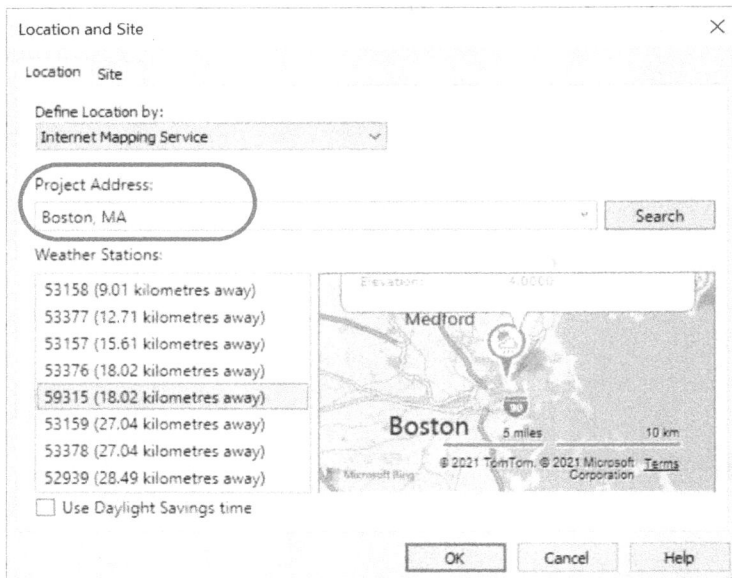

Figure 3–83

4. In the *Analyze* tab>Energy Optimization panel, click 🗔 (Energy Settings).

5. In the Energy Settings dialog box, set the *Mode* to **Use Rooms or Spaces**, as shown in Figure 3–84.

Figure 3–84

6. In the *Advanced* section, click the **Edit...** button next to *Other Options*.

7. In the Advanced Energy Settings dialog box, in the *Building Data* section, set the *Building Type* to **School or University** and the *Building Operating Schedule* to **K-12 School**, as shown in Figure 3–85.

8. In the *Room/Space Data* section, verify the *Export Category* is set to **Spaces**, as shown in Figure 3–85.

Figure 3–85

9. Click **OK** to close the Advanced Energy Settings dialog box.

10. Click **OK** to close the Energy Settings dialog box.

Task 2: Create the energy analytical model and review analytical spaces.

1. In the *Analyze* tab>Energy Optimization panel, click ⬚ (Create Energy Model).

2. The Create Energy Model dialog box will open notifying you that it may take considerable time to process the model, as shown in Figure 3–86. Click **Create the Energy Analytical Model**.

Create Energy Model – May Take Considerable Time   ✕

You are about to create the Energy Analytical Model. This may take considerable time during which Revit will not be accessible. What do you want to do?

→ Create the Energy Analytical Model

☐ Do not show me this message again.   Cancel

Click here to learn more

Figure 3–86

• During this exercise and depending on the computer, it may take from a few seconds to a few minutes to create the analytical model.

3. Once the model has processed, it will open the **Analytical Spaces** view, as shown in Figure 3–87. The view will also be found in the Project Browser under the Mechanical>???>3D Views node.

Figure 3–87

4. Review the Analytical Spaces view, then select one of the analytical spaces.

5. In Properties, review the analytical space's properties. Note that the spaces cannot be modified. This must be done when setting up the spaces.

6. Press <F9> to open the System Browser.

7. In the System Browser, select **Analytical Systems** in the drop-down list. If needed, expand **Unassigned**. You can select an analytical space(s) from the list and review its properties, as shown in Figure 3–88.

Figure 3–88

Task 3: Export to gbXML.

1. To export the analytical model to gbXML, in the *File* tab, expand ⬚ (Export) and click ⬚ (gbXML).

2. In the Create Analytical Spaces dialog box (shown in Figure 3–89), choose **Use Rooms/Spaces Elements** as the elements/mode to use for the export.

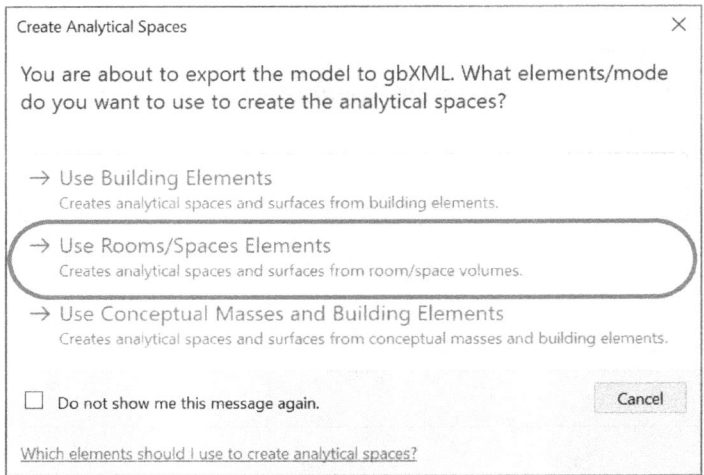

Create Analytical Spaces

You are about to export the model to gbXML. What elements/mode do you want to use to create the analytical spaces?

→ Use Building Elements
Creates analytical spaces and surfaces from building elements.

→ Use Rooms/Spaces Elements
Creates analytical spaces and surfaces from room/space volumes.

→ Use Conceptual Masses and Building Elements
Creates analytical spaces and surfaces from conceptual masses and building elements.

☐ Do not show me this message again.   Cancel

Which elements should I use to create analytical spaces?

Figure 3–89

3. In the Export gbXML - Save to Target Folder dialog box, select your practice files *MEP* folder for the folder location, keep the default file name, and click **Save**.

4. Open **Mech-Analysis.xml** from your practice files *MEP* folder and review the XML file, as shown in Figure 3–90.

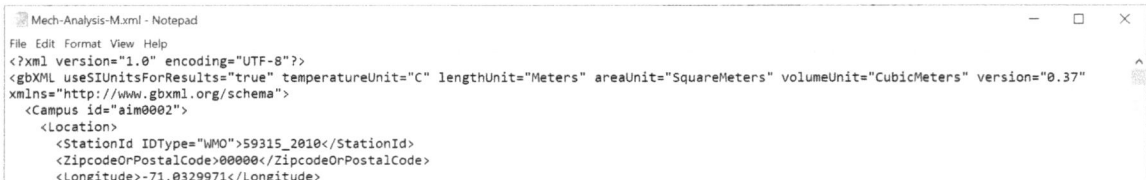

```
Mech-Analysis-M.xml - Notepad                                              —    □    ×
File  Edit  Format  View  Help
<?xml version="1.0" encoding="UTF-8"?>
<gbXML useSIUnitsForResults="true" temperatureUnit="C" lengthUnit="Meters" areaUnit="SquareMeters" volumeUnit="CubicMeters" version="0.37"
xmlns="http://www.gbxml.org/schema">
  <Campus id="aim0002">
    <Location>
      <StationId IDType="WMO">59315_2010</StationId>
      <ZipcodeOrPostalCode>00000</ZipcodeOrPostalCode>
      <Longitude>-71.0329971</Longitude>
```

Figure 3–90

5. Close the XML file.

6. Save and close the project.

End of practice

Chapter Review Questions

1. Which of the following types of CAD files can you import into Revit? (Select all that apply.)
   a. DGN
   b. DWG
   c. DOC
   d. DXF

2. Which of the following settings can be specified before you import AutoCAD files or Microstation files into a project?
   a. Color to Line Weight
   b. Text and Dimension Styles
   c. Units
   d. Patterns

3. Once a CAD file is imported into a Revit project, can you change the visibility of elements in the imported instance?
   a. Yes
   b. No

4. When you explode an imported instance of a CAD file, what type of elements would notes change to?
   a. Note Blocks
   b. Lines and Arcs
   c. Text
   d. Groups

5. Which of the following can you use to modify a raster image, such as the one shown in Figure 3–91? (Select all that apply.)

Figure 3–91

a. Delete portions of the graphic.

b. Resize it by dragging the corners.

c. Query the information inside the graphic.

d. Change the foreground/background status.

6. Which of the following settings can be specified when you export a project to DWG/DXF? (Select all that apply.)

a. Line Weight to Color

b. Text

c. Units

d. Patterns

7. (Optional) What elements MUST be in an architectural project before exporting to gbXML for energy analysis?

a. Ceilings

b. Floors

c. Rooms

d. Roofs

Command Summary

Button	Command	Location
Non-Revit Files		
	Coordination Model	• **Ribbon:** *Insert* tab>Link panel
	Delete Layers	• **Ribbon**: *Modify	[imported file name]* tab>Import Instance panel
	Explode	• **Ribbon**: *Modify	[imported file name]* tab>Import Instance panel
	Full Explode	• **Ribbon**: *Modify	[imported file name]* tab>Import Instance panel>Explode
	Import CAD	• **Ribbon**: *Insert* tab>Import panel
	Link CAD	• **Ribbon:** *Insert* tab>Link panel
	Partial Explode	• **Ribbon**: *Modify	[imported file name]* tab>Import Instance panel>Explode
	Query	• **Ribbon**: *Modify	[imported file name]* tab>Import Instance panel
	Scale	• **Ribbon**: *Modify* tab>Modify panel
Raster Files		
	Bring Forward	• **Ribbon**: *Modify	Raster Images* tab>Arrange panel
	Bring to Front	• **Ribbon**: *Modify	Raster Images* tab>Arrange panel
	Import Image	• **Ribbon**: *Insert* tab>Import panel
	Import PDF	• **Ribbon**: *Insert* tab>Import panel
	Link Image	• **Ribbon**: *Insert* tab>Link panel
	Link PDF	• **Ribbon**: *Insert* tab>Link panel

Button	Command	Location
	Manage Images	• **Ribbon**: *Insert* tab>Import panel
	Send Backward	• **Ribbon**: *Modify	Raster Images* tab>Arrange panel
	Send to Back	• **Ribbon**: *Modify	Raster Images* tab>Arrange panel

Energy Optimization

Button	Command	Location
	Location	• **Ribbon:** *Analyze* tab>Energy Optimization panel
	Energy Settings	• **Ribbon:** *Analyze* tab>Energy Optimization panel
	Create Energy Model	• **Ribbon:** *Analyze* tab>Energy Optimization panel
	Delete Energy Model	• **Ribbon:** *Analyze* tab>Energy Optimization panel

Exporting

Button	Command	Location
	ACIS (SAT)	• *File* **tab:** Expand Export>CAD Formats
	CAD Formats	• *File* **tab:** Expand Export
	DGN	• *File* **tab:** Expand Export>CAD Formats
	DWF/DWFx	• *File* **tab:** Expand Export
	DWG	• *File* **tab:** Expand Export>CAD Formats
	DXF	• *File* **tab:** Expand Export>CAD Formats
	Export	• *File* **tab**
	Export Setups DGN	• *File* **tab:** Expand Export>Options
	Export Setups DWG/DWF	• *File* **tab:** Expand Export>Options

Button	Command	Location
	Family Types	• *File* **tab:** Expand Export
	FBX	• *File* **tab:** Expand Export
	gbXML	• *File* **tab:** Expand Export
	IFC	• *File* **tab:** Expand Export
	IFC Options	• *File* **tab:** Expand Export>Options
	Images and Animations	• *File* **tab:** Expand Export
	ODBC Database	• *File* **tab:** Expand Export
	Options	• *File* **tab:** Expand Export
	Reports	• *File* **tab:** Expand Export

Project Team Collaboration

Project team collaboration happens on many levels in a firm and between disciplines. When you have a very large project with more than one person working on that project at one time, you need to enable worksharing, then create and use worksets. Worksets enable you to work in one part of a project while someone else is working in another part of the same project. Not everyone needs to know how to create a central model or set up worksets, but everyone needs to learn how to work with them.

Learning Objectives

- Understand worksharing workflow and definitions.
- Set up worksets in a project.
- Place elements in worksets.
- Create a central model.
- Create and open a local file based on the central model.
- Control workset visibility by view.
- Synchronize a local file with the central model.
- Set the active workset and work in the local file.
- Request and approve permission to edit elements.
- Temporarily enable the display of worksets.
- Close the workshared project correctly.
- Investigate tips for using worksets.

    Note: *The methodologies covered in this chapter focus on using server-based tools within Revit.*

4.1 Introduction to Worksharing

Note: *All images in the upcoming sections refer to users as "User1" or "User2". In your working environment, you will see your unique Revit username in these dialog boxes.*

Revit projects include the entire building model in one file. A process called *worksharing* is used when the file needs to be separated into logical components (as shown in Figure 4–1) without losing the connection to the whole. The main component of worksharing is worksets.

Worksharing gives multiple team members who are connected on the same network the ability to co-author a single project model (one RVT file). The appropriate team member creates a central model and worksets. Team members open and work in a local copy of the central model that is linked back to the central model through saving and synchronizing.

Worksharing in the cloud can also be done through Autodesk Docs, but this guide focuses on collaborating within your local area network.

Figure 4–1

A workshared project consists of one central model (also known as a central file) and individual models for each user known as local files, as shown in Figure 4–2. Each team member will work in their local file and use a function called *synchronizing with central* to send and receive updates with the central model.

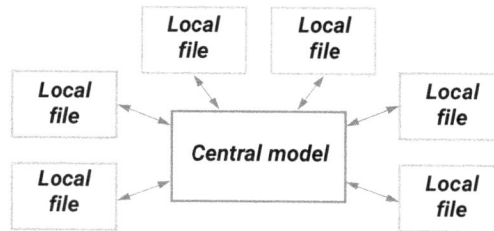

Figure 4-2

- The **central model** is created by the BIM manager, project manager, or project lead and is stored on a server or in the cloud, enabling multiple users to access it.

- A **local file** is a copy of the central model that is stored on your computer.

- All local files are saved back to the central model, and updates to the central model are sent out to the local files. This way, all changes remain in one file, while the project, model, views, and sheets are automatically updated.

Collaborate Tab

The tools found in the *Collaborate* tab, shown in Figure 4-3, are designed to help you and your team work more effectively in a workshared environment. Many of these tools are also available in the Quick Access Toolbar and Status Bar.

Figure 4-3

Worksharing Definitions

- **Worksharing:** This is a functionality that, when enabled, allows multiple members of the team to access a project stored in one centralized location, which gives multiple users the ability to work on the same project simultaneously.

- **Workshared file:** This is a project that has worksets enabled. If the project has no worksets enabled, it is called a *non-workshared file*.

- **Workset:** This is a collection of elements that are related geometrically, parametrically, or by location within an overall project that are subdivided so they can be worked on while isolated from the rest of the model. When worksharing is enabled, worksets are automatically activated and the *Workset1* and *Shared Levels and Grids* worksets are added to the project by default.

- **Central model:** Also called the central file, this is the main project file that is stored on a local network that all users can access. Using a central model is called *file-based worksharing*. The central model stores workset and element information in the project and is the file to which everyone saves and synchronizes their changes. The central model updates all the local files with the latest model information. This file should not be edited directly.

- **Local file:** This is a copy of the central model that is saved to your local computer. This is the file that you modify and work in. As you work, you save the file locally and synchronize it with the central model.

- **Element borrowing:** This refers to the process of modifying items in the project that are not part of the workset you have checked out. This either happens automatically (if no one else has checked out a workset) or specifically, when you request to have control of the elements (if someone else has a workset checked out).

- **Active workset:** The workset that displays in the Status Bar is the active workset. Any new elements that are added will be placed on this workset. As you work, you will change the active workset accordingly.

- **Relinquish:** This releases or returns a checked-out workset so that others can work on the elements within that workset. If you do not release or relinquish your checked-out worksets, other users will get a warning that they cannot edit the workset until you relinquish it, and they are given the option to request to borrow the workset. **Relinquish All Mine** allows you to relinquish worksets without synchronizing to the central model.

- **Reload Latest:** This updates your local file without you needing to synchronize with the central model.

General Process of Worksharing and Worksets

1. Wait for the appropriate team member to enable worksharing, set up worksets, and create the central model.

2. Create a local file from the central model.

3. Work in your local file and select the worksets that you need to work on by verifying the active workset.

   - Work in your local model by adding, deleting, and modifying elements.
   - You may need to request to borrow elements in worksets that are currently checked out by other team members.

4. Save the local file as frequently as you would save any other project.

5. Synchronize the local file with the central model several times a day or as required by company policy or project status.

   - This reloads any changes from the central model to your local file and vice versa.
   - If the option to **Save Local File before and after synchronizing with central** is checked, your local file will be saved, but it is always recommended to save the local file yourself every time you synchronize to the central model.

4.2 Enabling Worksharing

Once it has been established that a project will need to be workshared, a designated person will enable worksharing, create worksets, and create the central model. The central model will be placed in a shared centralized network location and each user will create their own local file to work from. The central model will host all updated information for the project so that it can be distributed to each user as it is updated.

How To: Enable Worksharing

1. Open an existing project that will become your workshared file or start a new project.

2. In the *Collaborate* tab>Manage Collaboration panel, click ⬚ (Collaborate).

    *   If this file has never been saved or if changes have been made and not yet saved, the Collaborate - Revit Model Not Saved dialog box will display, as shown in Figure 4–4. Select **Save the model and continue**.

Collaborate - Revit Model Not Saved   ✕
You have to save the model before you can collaborate with others. Would you like to save the model?
→ Save the model and continue
→ Don't save the model and cancel

    Figure 4–4

    *   In the Save As dialog box, save the model to a shared network location for everyone to access it.

3. In the Collaborate dialog box, select **Within your network**, as shown in Figure 4−5, and click **OK**.

Figure 4−5

4. Once worksharing is enabled, default worksets will be created in the model.

5. In the *File* tab, expand 💾 (Save As) and click ✉ (Project).

6. In the Save As dialog box, click **Options...** and verify that **Central file** is checked.

7. The **Make this a Central Model after save** option is selected but grayed out. This project must become the central model because you have initiated worksets. Click **OK** to close the dialog box.

•   Worksharing in the cloud can be done through Autodesk Docs, but this guide focuses on collaborating within your local area network.

Hint: Central Model Indicator

On the Home screen within the thumbnail views of the recent project, there is an indicator icon (⬚) that designates that the model is a central model, as shown on the left in Figure 4–6. The model on the right is not a central model, so it has no indicator icon.

Elementary-School-MEP.r...   Elementary-School-MEP

Figure 4–6

This serves as a reminder that central models should generally not be opened directly to be edited, but rather should be used to create a local file through the File Open dialog box, as shown in Figure 4–7. Note that within this dialog box there is no indicator that a file is a central model.

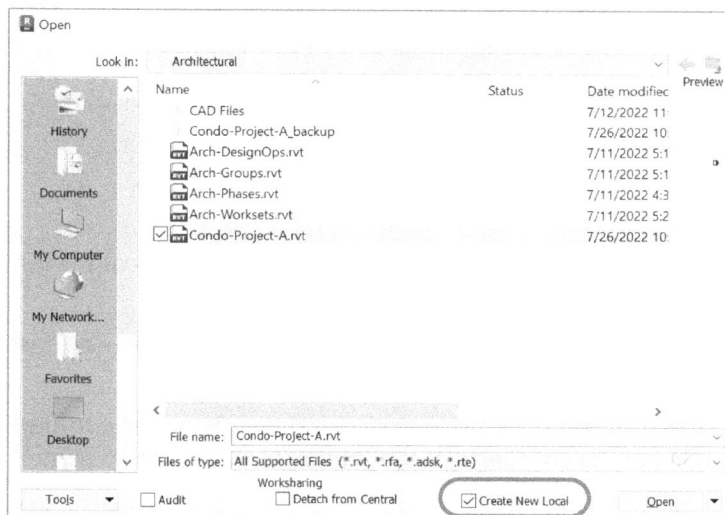

Figure 4–7

4.3 Setting Up Worksets

After a project has worksharing enabled, worksets need to be created. Individual worksets are subsets of a project with only specific elements available to view or edit per team member. Worksets are created in the Worksets dialog box, as shown in Figure 4–8. There are four categories of worksets: User-Created, Families, Project Standards, and Views.

Figure 4–8

- It is important to have one user start a project and develop most of the views, families, and other settings before sharing.

- If you have multiple buildings in a project, use linking to show the relationships between the buildings. Each Revit model can have its own worksets.

- Determining how to divide a project into worksets depends on the complexity of the project, the need to be able to load only parts of the model, and the need to control visibility by workset.

- If your company's BIM standards are to primarily check out worksets rather than borrowing on the fly, dividing the project depends on the different tasks to be done and the number of people working on the project. See "Best Practices for Worksharing" on page 92.

- User-Created worksets should be based on areas of the building that can be worked on when isolated from the rest of the model, such as the exterior shell, building core, or certain sections of the building that can be worked on by a single user at a time.

- You can also have worksets for electrical, site, and structural work that are not visible to other users, and separate worksets for linked Revit files.

How To: Create Worksets

1. In the *Collaborate* tab>Manage Collaboration panel, click (Worksets). Alternatively, in the Status Bar, click (Worksets).

   - Two default User-Created worksets are created: *Shared Levels and Grids* and *Workset1*.
   - Four categories of worksets are created by default, as described below:

Workset Category	Definition
User-Created	User-Created worksets are used to divide the overall model into collections of elements that are related, usually geometrically, so that the elements can be edited by a user as if they were isolated from the rest of the model.
Families	Each family type loaded into a project will have its own workset. This prevents type changes from being made to a family that is also being used by another user, even if you are using separate worksets. Family worksets cannot be renamed or deleted.
Project Standards	Project Standards are overall project settings, such as system family types (walls, ceilings, roofs, etc.), filters, fill patterns, line styles, materials, or text types. Project Standards worksets help keep these things consistent while multiple people are working on a collaborated model and allow more than one user to work with them at the same time.
Views	Every view that exists in a project will also have its own workset, which allows for any annotation or drafting elements to be placed in the View workset rather than in a workset with model elements. This happens automatically, so there is no need to specify the correct workset when you are placing annotation elements.

2. In the Worksets dialog box, click **New**. In the New Workset dialog box, type a name for the workset, as shown in Figure 4–9, and click **OK**.

Figure 4–9

- As they are created, the worksets are open and editable by the person who set them up.

- Select or clear the **Visible in all views** option, as needed. For example, a workset showing the exterior of the building is required in all views, while a furniture layout is only required in specific views.

3. Continue to create new worksets, as needed.

4. Set the *Active workset*. This designates which workset will be active, meaning any new elements added to the project will be part of this workset.

- Selecting the **Gray Inactive Workset Graphics** checkbox allows users to have a visual understanding of which elements in a project are active and inactive by graying out inactive worksets.

- The new worksets are automatically made **Editable**.

- You can change existing workset names in the Worksets dialog box. Select the workset and click **Rename**.

  - You can rename the default Workset1 workset.

  - You cannot rename the default Project Standards, Families, or Views worksets.

- If you delete a workset and there are elements in the workset, the Delete Workset dialog box (shown in Figure 4–10) displays, prompting you to choose what to do with any elements in the workset. They can either be deleted or moved to another workset.

Figure 4–10

- To rename or delete a workset, it must first be made editable.
  - The Workset1, Project Standards, Families, and Views worksets cannot be deleted.
5. Click **OK** to close the dialog box.

Placing Elements in Worksets

When you are working with an existing model that has worksharing enabled and worksets created, you will want to place existing building elements into the appropriate worksets. For example, move any furniture already in a project to a furniture workset, as shown in Figure 4–11.

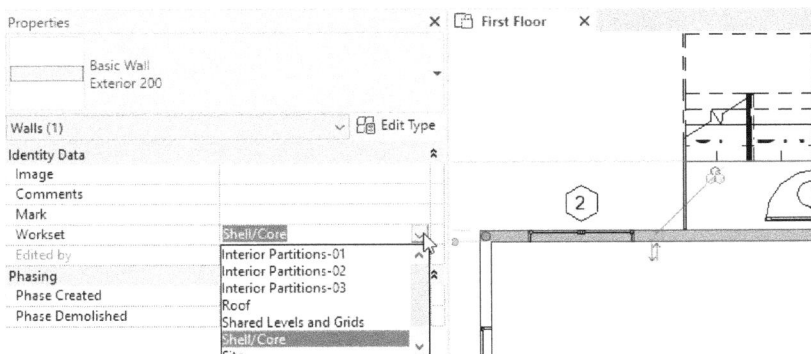

Figure 4–11

- Worksets can span levels; therefore, you can select elements on each level and move them into the appropriate workset.

- Whatever elements are not moved will remain in the default workset, which is Workset1.

How To: Move Elements to the Appropriate Worksets

1. Open a view that displays the elements you need to move to a different workset.

2. Select the element(s).

3. In Properties, change the *Workset* parameter to the workset in which you want the elements to be, as shown previously in Figure 4–11.

- You can select multiple types of building elements and move them to a workset. However, you will need to filter out any annotation elements, such as views and tags, that are automatically assigned to the related View workset.

- Curtain wall subcomponents (grids, mullions, and panels) must be filtered out of a selection set. Select just the base curtain wall element when you want to move it to a workset.

- If you have added elements to a workset that is not visible in the current workset, the elements do not display in the view. If you need elements to be visible, open the Visibility/ Graphic Overrides dialog box. Select the *Worksets* tab and modify the *Visibility Setting* for the worksets you want to be visible in the current view, as shown in Figure 4–12.

Worksets	Visibility Setting
Exterior Shell	Use Global Setting (Visible)
Furniture	Use Global Setting (Visible)
Plumbing	Use Global Setting (Not Visible)
Shared Levels and Grids	Use Global Setting (Visible)

Figure 4–12

💡 Hint: Setting a Starting View

To save time when opening a complex model with worksharing activated, you can specify a *starting view*. This could be a cover sheet or a drafting view with information about the project. The idea is that the contents of the starting view are simple elements rather than model elements.

- To set the starting view, in the *Manage* tab>Manage Project panel, click 🔲 (Starting View). In the Starting View dialog box, select the view name, as shown in Figure 4–13.

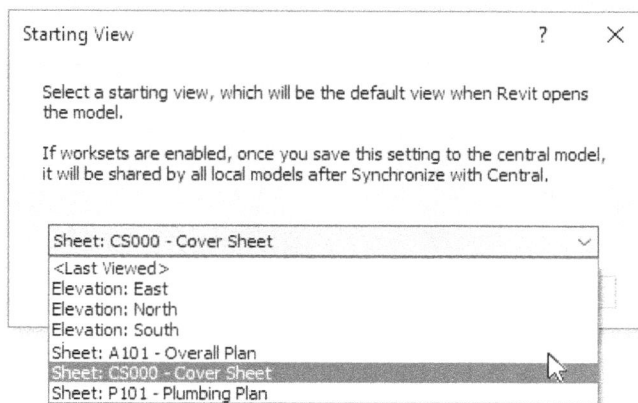

Figure 4–13

4.4 Create a Central Model

The central model keeps track of available worksets and coordinates the changes made in each one with the rest of the worksets. It needs to be accessible to all team members, but should not be worked in directly. The central model maintains a connection to all local files and distributes updated information when a user syncs or reloads latest.

How To: Create a Central Model

1. In the workshared project's *File* tab, click 🖫 (Save As)> 🗀 (Project).

2. In the Save As dialog box, navigate to the network location and click the **Options...** button.

3. In the File Save Options dialog box, **Make this a Central Model after save** is selected and grayed out (as shown Figure 4–14) because worksets have been enabled and the next step is to create the central model. Click **OK**.

Figure 4–14

4. In the Quick Access Toolbar or the *Collaborate* tab> Synchronize panel, click

    🖫 (Synchronize and Modify Settings).

5. In the Synchronize with Central dialog box, select **User-created Worksets**, as shown in Figure 4–15, so that worksets you checked out are relinquished and available to everyone. You can also add a comment. Click **OK**.

Figure 4–15

6. Close the central model.

Practice 4a
Set Up a Workshared File - Architectural

Practice Objectives

- Enable worksharing on an existing project.
- Set up worksets and move existing elements to the worksets.
- Create a central model.

In this practice, you will set up a workshared file from an existing project, create worksets, move building elements to different worksets, and create a central model.

Task 1: Set up a workshared file.

1. Verify no projects are open. On the Home screen, in the *MODELS* section, click **Open....** In the practice files *Architectural* folder, open **Arch-Worksets-M.rvt**.

2. In the *Collaborate* tab>Manage Collaboration panel, click 🖼 (Collaborate).

3. In the Collaborate dialog box, select **Within your network** and click **OK**.

4. In the *Collaborate* tab>Manage Collaboration panel or in the Status Bar, click 🐾 (Worksets).

5. In the Worksets dialog box, select **Workset1** and click **Rename**.

6. In the Rename dialog box, rename Workset1 to **Exterior** and click **OK**.

- When you have an existing project and you are creating worksets, you want to rename Workset1 to something that the project has a majority of. For example, an architectural project will have a lot of walls, doors, and windows; therefore, you would want all the elements to start out in this workset instead of trying to pick all the elements individually to put in the appropriate workset.

7. In the Worksets dialog box, click **New**.

8. In the New Workset dialog box, enter **Furniture Level 1** for the new workset name, uncheck **Visible in all views** (as shown in Figure 4–16), and click **OK**.

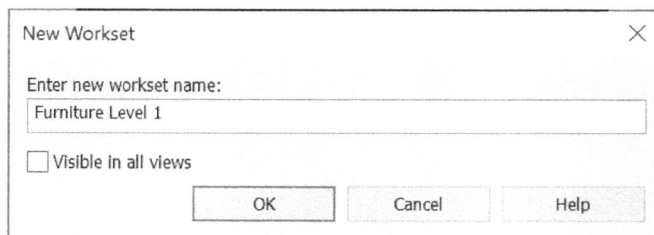

New Workset	✕
Enter new workset name:	
Furniture Level 1	
☐ Visible in all views	
OK Cancel Help	

Figure 4–16

9. Create additional new worksets using the names and **Visible in all views** option settings shown in the table below.

New workset name	Visible in all views
Interior Level 1	unchecked
Interior Level 2	unchecked
Plumbing Fixtures	checked
Vertical Circulation	checked

Note: Owner "User1" will differ for each user and will be your Revit username, found in Options in the General pane.

10. Verify that the *Active workset* is **Exterior**. Select **Gray Inactive Workset Graphics** (as shown in Figure 4–17) and click **OK** to close the Worksets dialog box. (Note: Your workset name order may differ from the one shown.)

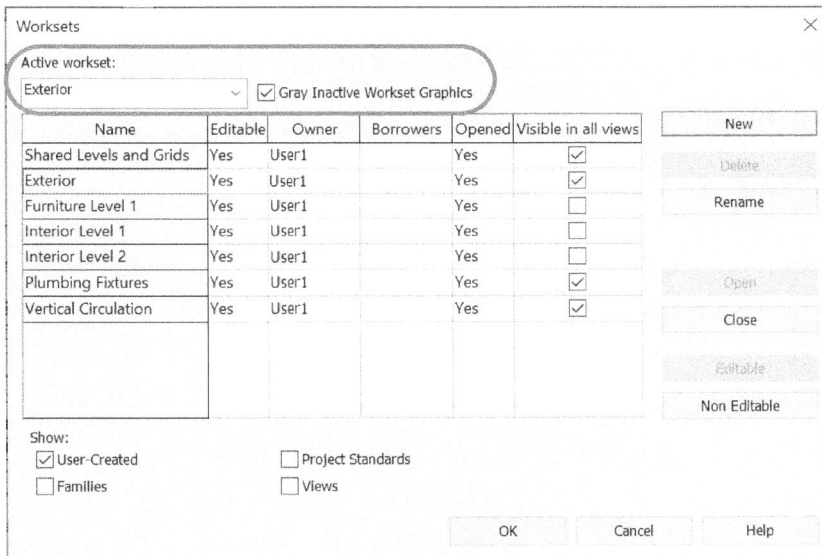

Figure 4–17

11. When prompted to change the active workset (as shown in Figure 4–18), click **No** to keep the Exterior workset active instead of the last workset you created.

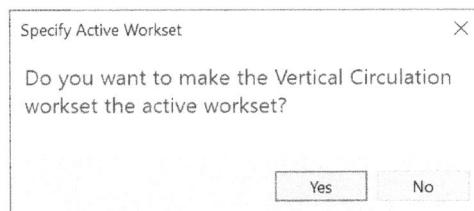

Figure 4–18

12. Elements on the Shared Levels and Grids workset and the view-specific room tags are grayed out. Everything in the Exterior workset displays in black.

   • You can check which workset is active either in the Status Bar or in the *Collaborate* tab> Manage Collaboration panel>Active Workset drop-down list, as shown in Figure 4–19.

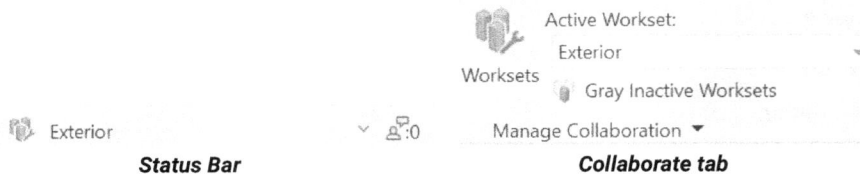

| Status Bar | Collaborate tab |

Figure 4–19

Task 2: Move building elements to worksets.

1. In the **Floor Plans: Level 1** view, select all of the interior walls, columns, and doors. Use (Filter) to remove other items from the selection set. Ensure that you do not select any exterior doors, rooms, room tags, and especially the curtain wall door.

2. In Properties, change the *Workset* for the selected elements to **Interior Level 1**. The items should be removed from the view if you toggled off the **Visible by default** option when you created the workset.

3. Repeat the process for the following elements. These elements are still visible but grayed out, as shown in Figure 4–20.

Elements	Workset
• Furniture • Furniture systems	**Furniture Level 1**
• Elevators (Specialty Equipment) • Stairs • Railing	**Vertical Circulation**
• Bathroom items	**Plumbing Fixtures**

Figure 4–20

4. Select an exterior wall. Note that the workset is **Exterior**.

5. Click **Modify**.

Task 3: Create a central model.

1. In the *File* tab, expand 💾 (Save As) and click 📁 (Project). In the Save As dialog box, click **Options...** and verify that **Central file** is checked.

    - The **Make this a Central Model after save** option is selected but grayed out. This project must become the central model because you have initiated worksets. Click **OK** to close the dialog box.

    Note: For this practice, you will be saving to your local drive, but central models must always be saved to a network location.

2. Name the file **Arch-Worksets-M.rvt** and be sure that you are saving it within your practice files *Architectural* folder. Click **Save**. Click **Yes** in the Replace Existing File dialog box.

3. In the Status Bar, click 🗗 (Worksets). All of the files are now *Editable* with your username listed as the *Owner*, as shown in Figure 4–21.

Name	Editable	Owner	Borrowers	Opened	Visible in all views
Exterior	Yes	User1		Yes	☑
Furniture Level 1	Yes	User1		Yes	☐
Interior Level 1	Yes	User1		Yes	☐
Interior Level 2	Yes	User1		Yes	☐
Plumbing Fixtures	Yes	User1		Yes	☑
Shared Levels and Grids	Yes	User1		Yes	☑
Vertical Circulation	Yes	User1		Yes	☑

Figure 4–21

4. Click **OK** to close the dialog box.

5. In the *Collaborate* tab>Synchronize panel, click 🗗 (Synchronize and Modify Settings). In the Synchronize with Central dialog box, select the option to relinquish **User-created Worksets** so that they are available to everyone, as shown in Figure 4–22.

Note: Since no local file has been created from this model, the "Save Local File before and after synchronizing with central" option is grayed out.

Figure 4–22

6. Click **OK** to synchronize with central and close the file.

End of practice

Practice 4b
Set Up a Workshared File - Structural

Practice Objectives

- Enable worksharing on an existing project.
- Set up worksets and move existing elements to the worksets.
- Create a central model.

In this practice, you will set up a workshared file from an existing project, set up worksets, move elements to different worksets, and create a central model.

Task 1: Set up a workshared file.

1. Verify no projects are open. On the Home screen, in the *MODELS* section, click **Open....** In the practice files *Structural* folder, open **Struct-Worksets-M.rvt**.

2. In the *Collaborate* tab>Manage Collaboration panel, click 🖫 (Collaborate).

3. In the Collaborate dialog box, select **Within your network** and click **OK**.

4. In the *Collaborate* tab>Manage Collaboration panel or in the Status Bar, click 🗊 (Worksets).

5. In the Worksets dialog box, select **Workset1** and click **Rename**.

6. In the Rename dialog box, rename Workset1 as **Columns, Beams & Bracing** and click **OK**.

- When you have an existing project and you are creating worksets, you want to rename Workset1 to something that the project has a majority of. For example, a structural project will have a lot of columns, beams, and bracing; therefore, you would want all the elements to start out in this workset instead of trying to pick all columns, beams, and bracing to put in the appropriate workset.

7. In the Worksets dialog box, click **New**.

8. In the New Workset dialog box, enter **Core Walls** as the new workset name, uncheck **Visible in all views** (as shown in Figure 4–23), and click **OK**.

Figure 4–23

9. Create additional new worksets using the names and **Visible in all views** option settings shown in the table below.

New workset name	Visible in all views
Foundation	unchecked
Slab and Roofs	unchecked

Note: Owner "User1" will differ for each user and will be your Revit username, found in Options in the General pane.

10. Verify that the *Active workset* is **Columns, Beams & Bracing**, as shown in Figure 4–24. Select **Gray Inactive Workset Graphics** and click **OK** to close the Worksets dialog box. (Note: Your workset name order may differ from the one shown.)

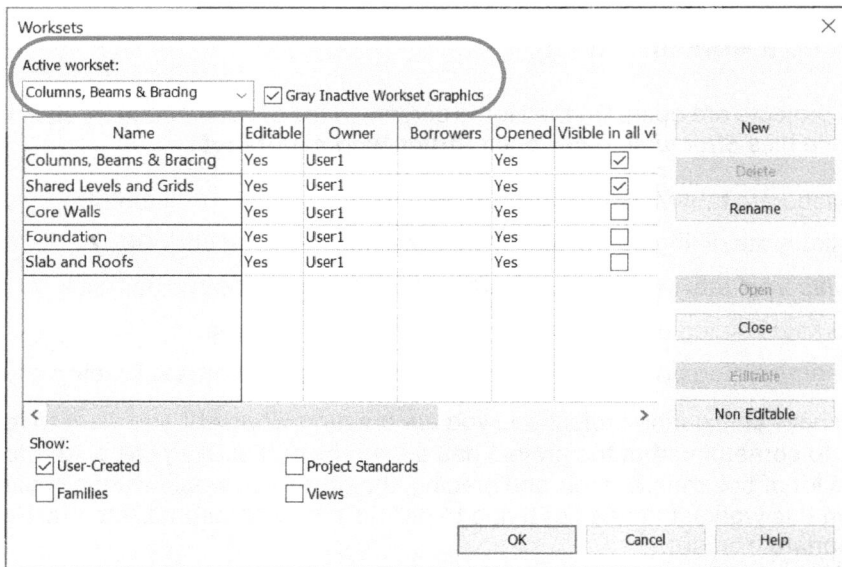

Figure 4–24

11. When prompted to change the active workset (as shown in Figure 4–25), click **No** to keep the active workset as Columns, Beams & Bracing instead of the last workset you created.

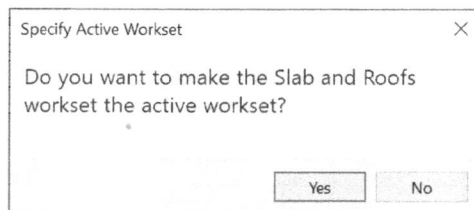

Figure 4–25

- You can check which workset is active either in the Status Bar or in the *Collaborate* tab> Manage Collaboration panel>Active Workset drop-down list, as shown in Figure 4–26.

Active Workset:
Columns, Beams & Bracing
Worksets
Gray Inactive Worksets

Columns, Beams _Bracing &:0   Manage Collaboration ▾

Status Bar   **Collaborate tab**

Figure 4–26

12. Open the **Structural Plans: Level 1** view. Elements in the Shared Levels and Grids workset and the view-specific view and section markers are grayed out. Everything else is black because they are in the Columns, Beams & Bracing workset that was formerly named Workset1.

Task 2: Move building elements to worksets.

1. Open the **Elevations (Building Elevation): East** view.

2. Select all of the elements from Level 1 down to the lowest footing, as shown in Figure 4–27, using a selection window from left to right.

Figure 4–27

3. In Properties, change the workset for the selected elements to **Foundation**.

   - Although you are changing the workset for the wall foundations, analytical wall foundations do not automatically follow and it is not possible to manually change their workset. When starting a project from scratch, as would typically be the case, it is important to set the right workset before creating the wall foundations.

4. In the East Elevation, select everything from the penthouse level down to level 1 in the view.

   Use ▽ (Filter) to only select the slabs (floors), slab edge, and roofs. Move them to the **Slabs & Roofs** workset.

5. In the warning dialog box, click **Unjoin Elements**, as shown in Figure 4–28.

Autodesk Revit

Warning   --   0 Errors, 3 Warnings

One element is completely inside another.

<<   1 of 3   >>   Show   More Info   Expand >>

Unjoin Elements   OK   Cancel

Figure 4–28

6. Repeat the procedure by drawing a selection window around the elevator masonry walls.

Use ▽ (Filter) to only select the shaft openings and walls, as shown in Figure 4–29, and add them to the **Core Walls** workset.

Figure 4–29

Task 3: Create a central model.

1. In the *File* tab, expand 💾 (Save As) and click 📁 (Project).

   Note: *For this practice, you will be saving to your local drive, but central models must always be saved to a network location.*

2. In the Save As dialog box, click **Options...**. The **Make this a Central Model after save** option is selected but grayed out. This project must become the central model because you have initiated worksets. Click **OK** to close the dialog box.

3. Name the file **Struct-Worksets-M.rvt** and be sure that you are saving it within your practice files *Structural* folder. Click **Save**. Click **Yes** in the Replace Existing File dialog box.

4. Click (Worksets). All of the files are listed as *Editable* with your username listed as the *Owner*, as shown in Figure 4–30.

Name	Editable	Owner	Borrowers	Opened	Visible in all vi	
Columns, Beams & Bracing	Yes	User1		Yes	☑	
Core Walls	Yes	User1		Yes	☐	
Foundation	Yes	User1		Yes	☐	
Shared Levels and Grids	Yes	User1		Yes	☑	
Slab and Roofs	Yes	User1		Yes	☐	

Figure 4–30

5. Click **OK** to close the dialog box.

6. Click (Synchronize and Modify Settings). In the Synchronize with Central dialog box, select the option to relinquish **User-created Worksets** so that they are available to everyone and add an appropriate comment, as shown in Figure 4–31.

Figure 4–31

7. Click **OK** to synchronize with central and close the file.

End of practice

Practice 4c
Set Up a Workshared File - MEP

Practice Objectives

- Enable worksharing on an existing project.
- Set up worksets and move existing elements to the worksets.
- Create a central model.

In this practice, you will set up a workshared file from an existing project, set up worksets, move building elements to different worksets, and create a central model.

Task 1: Set up a workshared file.

1. In the practice files *MEP* folder, open **Mech-Worksets-M.rvt**.

2. In the *Collaborate* tab>Manage Collaboration panel, click (Collaborate).

3. In the Collaborate dialog box, select **Within your network** and click **OK**.

4. In the *Collaborate* tab>Manage Collaboration panel or in the Status Bar, click (Worksets).

5. In the Worksets dialog box, select **Workset1** and click **Rename**.

6. In the Rename dialog box, rename Workset1 to **HVAC** and click **OK**.

   - When you have an existing project and you are creating worksets, you want to rename Workset1 to something that the project has a majority of. For example, a mechanical project will have a lot of ducts and duct fittings; therefore, you would want all the elements to start out in this workset instead of trying to pick all elements individually to put in the appropriate workset.

7. In Worksets dialog box, click **New**.

8. In the New Workset dialog box, enter **Data and Security** as the new workset name, uncheck **Visible in all views** (as shown in Figure 4–32), and click **OK**.

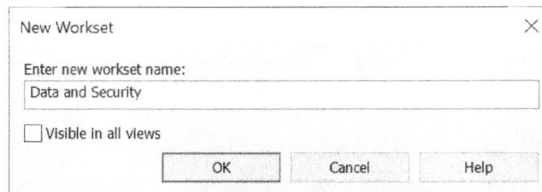

Figure 4–32

9. Create additional new worksets using the names and **Visible in all views** option settings shown in the table below.

New workset name	Visible in all views
Architectural Link	checked
Lighting	unchecked
Plumbing	unchecked

Note: Owner "User1" will differ for each user and will be your Revit username, found in Options in the General pane.

10. Verify that the active workset is **HVAC**. Select the **Gray Inactive Workset Graphics** option, as shown in Figure 4–33, and click **OK** to close the Worksets dialog box. (Note: Your workset name order may differ from the one shown.)

Figure 4–33

11. If prompted to change the active workset (as shown in Figure 4–34), click **No** to keep the HVAC workset active instead of the last workset you created.

Figure 4–34

- You can check which workset is active either in the Status Bar or in the *Collaborate* tab> Manage Collaboration panel>Active Workset drop-down list, as shown in Figure 4–35.

Active Workset:
HVAC
Worksets   Gray Inactive Worksets

HVAC   ⌄ ⏚:0   Manage Collaboration ▾

Status Bar   **Collaborate tab**

Figure 4–35

Task 2: Move building elements to worksets.

1. In the 3D view, select some of the ducts and equipment. In Properties, you can see that the *Workset* is **HVAC**.

2. Select the linked architectural model. In Properties, it is also set to HVAC. Change the *Workset* to **Architectural Link**.

   Note: If you cannot select the linked architectural model, in the Status Bar, click

   ⏚⤫ *(Select Links (off)) to toggle it on.*

3. Open the Electrical>Lighting>Floor Plans>**1-Lighting** view.

4. Select all of the lighting fixtures and move them to the **Lighting** workset. The elements are removed from the view because the Lighting workset is set to not visible.

   Note: Use ▽ *(Filter) to remove other items from the selection set, if needed.*

5. Open the Mechanical>Plumbing>Floor Plans>**1-Plumbing** view and move the plumbing fixtures to the **Plumbing** workset. These elements are also removed from the view because the Plumbing workset is set to not visible.

6. Open the Coordination>MEP>Floor Plans>**1 - MEP** view.

7. Open the Worksets dialog box and make the **Lighting** and **Plumbing** worksets visible. Check the checkbox next to **Gray Inactive Workset Graphics**. Click **OK**. The view displays with the HVAC workset in color but the other worksets grayed out, as shown in Figure 4–36.

Figure 4–36

Task 3: Create a central model.

1. In the *File* tab, expand ⬛ (Save As), and click 🖼 (Project).

   Note: For this practice, you will be saving to your local drive, but central models must always be saved to a network location.

2. In the Save As dialog box, click **Options....** The **Make this a Central Model after save** option is selected but grayed out. This project must become the central model because you have initiated worksets. Click **OK** to close the dialog box.

3. Make sure the name is **Mech-Worksets-M.rvt** and that you are saving it within your practice files *MEP* folder. Click **Save**. Click **Yes** in the Replace Existing File dialog box.

4. Click 🏢 (Worksets). All of the files are now *Editable* with your username listed as the *Owner*. Clear **Visible in all views** for *Lighting* and *Plumbing*, as shown in Figure 4–37.

Figure 4–37

5. Click **OK** to close the dialog box.

6. Click (Synchronize and Modify Settings). In the Synchronize with Central dialog box, select the option to relinquish **User-created Worksets** so that they are available to everyone and add an appropriate comment, as shown in Figure 4–38.

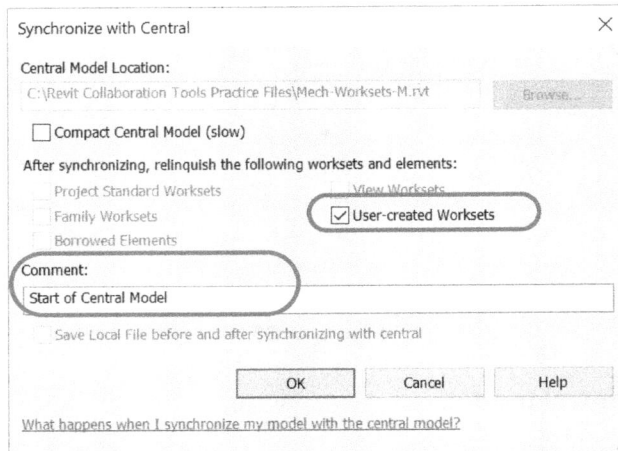

Figure 4–38

7. Click **OK** to synchronize with central and close the file.

End of practice

4.5 Create a Local File from a Central Model

After a central model has been saved to a shared local network location, you will use the Open dialog box to create a local copy, as shown in Figure 4–39. Doing this creates a link between your local file and the central model.

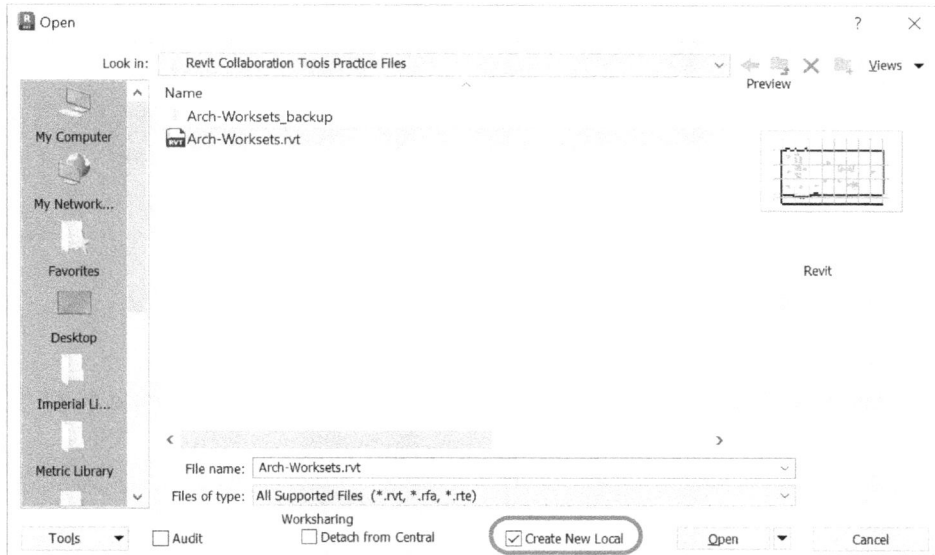

Figure 4–39

• You always work directly in your local file and synchronize your changes to the central model.

• Synchronizing to central will also update your local file with any changes from other users working on the project.

💡 Hint: Notifications and Default File Location

In the *File* tab, click **Options**. In the Options dialog box, in the *General* tab, you can set reminders to save and synchronize the local file with the central model, as shown in Figure 4–40.

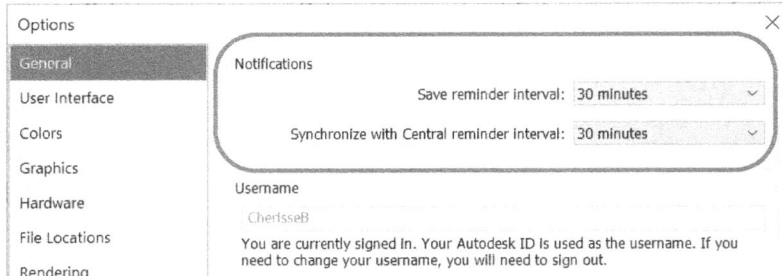

Figure 4–40

- This pane is also where your local file pulls your username from.

In the *File Locations* tab, set the *Default path for user files*, as shown in Figure 4–41.

Figure 4–41

- This pane is also where you set the location for project template files, family template files, and point cloud files.

How To: Create a Local File

1. In the Quick Access Toolbar, click ☐ (Open).

2. In the Open dialog box, navigate to the central model and verify that **Create New Local** (shown previously in Figure 4–39) is checked.

    There are two other options available in the Open dialog box:

    *   **Detach from Central:** Opens the file and detaches it from the central model. This should only be done by the administrator of the central model.
    *   **Audit:** Scans and fixes corrupt elements in a model when working with workshared files.

3. Click **Open**. You can also expand the **Open** button for other options, as shown in Figure 4–42 and explained in the following table.

Figure 4–42

All	Opens all worksets.
Editable	Opens all worksets that are editable (not checked out by someone else).
Last Viewed	Opens the worksets that were viewed the last time you saved the local file. This is the default setting after the local file has been saved once.
Specify	Opens the Opening Worksets dialog box (once you click **Open**), where you select the worksets you want opened or closed.

If you select **Specify...** and click **Open**, the Opening Worksets dialog box displays, as shown in Figure 4–43, where you can do the following:

- Select the name of the workset(s) and click **Close** if a workset is opened and you want it closed.
- Select the name of the workset(s) and click **Open** if a workset is closed and you want it opened.
- Select more than one workset by holding <Ctrl> or <Shift>.
- Select all of the worksets by pressing <Ctrl>+<A>.

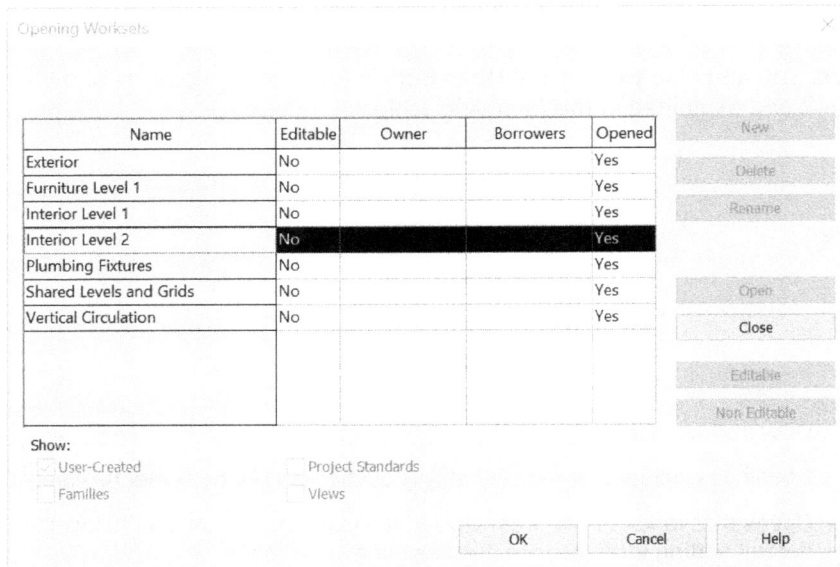

Figure 4–43

4. Click **OK** in the Opening Worksets dialog box after making your selections.

5. A copy of the project is created. It will have the same name as the central model with your Autodesk Revit username added to the end.

6. In the *Collaborate* tab>Synchronize panel, expand the Synchronize with Central drop-down list and select (Synchronize and Modify Settings).

7. In the Synchronize with Central dialog box, verify that the *Central Model Location* path is correct and that **Save Local File before and after synchronizing with central** is checked, as shown in Figure 4–44. You can add a comment if needed.

Figure 4–44

8. Click **OK** to close the dialog box.

- After your local file is created, you will not open the central model again unless a new local file is needed. You will always work from your local file.

- Save the local file as frequently as you would save any other project.

- Synchronize the local file with the central model several times a day or as required by company policy or project status.

  - If your company policy is to create a new local file daily or weekly, when you open the central model with **Create New Local** checked, you will get the Duplicate name dialog box, as shown in Figure 4–45. Click **Overwrite existing copy** to continue.

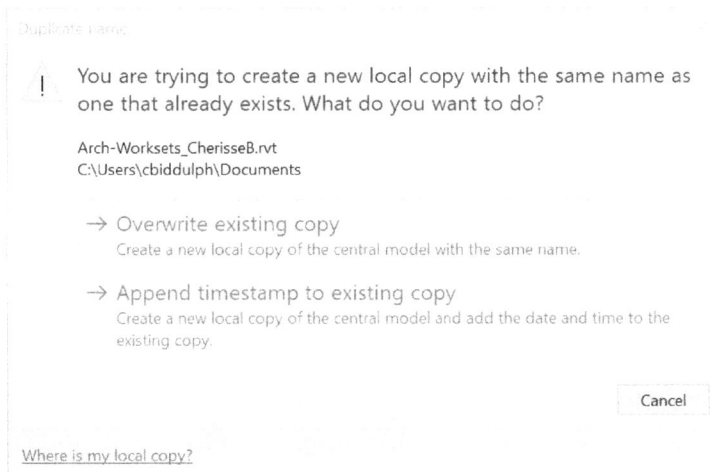

Figure 4–45

- **Append timestamp to existing copy** creates a new local file but adds the date and time to the end of the file name in your local file location, as shown in Figure 4–46.

Figure 4–46

- When you open a local file, select only the worksets you need to open. Limiting the number of worksets speeds up the opening and saving process and frees up elements for other project team members to edit.

Saving and Synchronizing Your Local File

To save your local file, you can click ![save icon] (Save) in the Quick Access Toolbar. You can also make sure that within the Synchronize with Central dialog box, you have the checkbox selected for **Save Local File before and after synchronizing with central**, as shown in Figure 4–47.

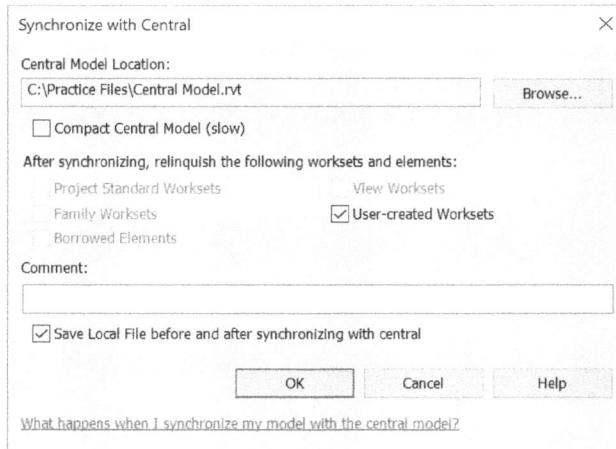

Figure 4–47

- Save the local file frequently (every 15 to 30 minutes).

- Synchronize to the central model periodically (every hour or two) or after you have made major changes to the project. At the end of the day, make sure you synchronize with central and relinquish worksets.

Synchronizing to the Central Model

There are two methods for synchronizing to the central model. In the Quick Access Toolbar or

Collaborate tab>Synchronize panel, expand [icon] (Synchronize with Central) and click

[icon] (Synchronize Now) or [icon] (Synchronize and Modify Settings). The last-used command is active if you click the top-level icon.

- **Synchronize Now:** Updates the central model and then the local file with any changes to the central model since the last synchronization without prompting you for any settings. It automatically relinquishes elements borrowed from any workset but retains worksets used by the current user.

- **Synchronize and Modify Settings:** Opens the Synchronize with Central dialog box so you can set the options for relinquishing worksets and elements, add comments, and specify to save the file locally before and after synchronization.

- Always keep **Save Local File before and after synchronizing with central** checked to ensure your local copy is up to date with the latest changes from the central model.

- When you close a local file without saving to the central model, you are prompted to do so, as shown in Figure 4–48.

Figure 4–48

4.6 Working in a Workshared File

The key to successfully working in a workshared project is coordinating and communicating with the other members of your team. However, the majority of the work you will do in a workshared project will be no different than any other project. Only check out worksets that you need to work in (as shown in Figure 4–49) and borrow elements as you work.

Figure 4–49

When new elements are added to the project, they are placed in the active workset, as shown in Figure 4–50. It is therefore important to set the active workset correctly before adding new elements. Not doing so can result in visibility and permissions-related issues.

<Workset: Element name> ⟶ Shell/Core : Walls : Basic Wall : Exterior - Brick on CMU : R32

Status Bar showing active workset ⟶ Shell/Core   ⌄ ⧸:0 ▦ ▤ Main Moc

Figure 4–50

How To: Set the Active Workset

1. Open your local file.

2. In the Status Bar (or *Collaborate* tab>Manage Collaboration panel), expand the *Active Workset* list and select a workset, as shown in Figure 4–51.

Figure 4–51

*   It does not matter if the workset says **(Not Editable)**; you can still add elements to it. **Not Editable** means that you have not checked out the workset but are working on the basis of borrowing elements.

*   You can gray out inactive worksets in a view to easily distinguish between active and inactive worksets, as shown in Figure 4–52. In the *Collaborate* tab>Manage Collaboration panel, toggle (Gray Inactive Workset Graphics) on. You can also select **Gray Inactive Workset Graphics** in the Worksets dialog box.

Figure 4–52

💡 Hint: Worksharing Monitoring

Worksharing monitoring displays information about the workshared model you are working in or have opened, as shown in Figure 4–53. It shows you who is working in the project, if there are any issues, if your local file is up to date, and information about requests for borrowing elements. You can also set up options on what information you would like displayed in desktop notifications that appear above your computer's system tray (Date and Time). You can click on the History icon to display the action from all team members working in the project.

Click to open the Central File History dialog box

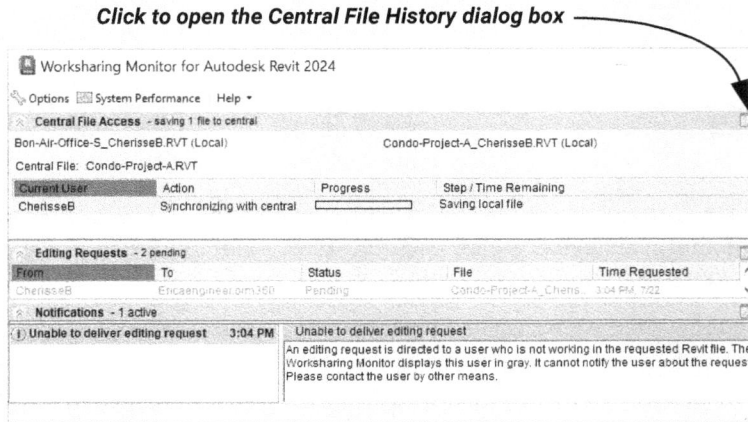

Figure 4–53

- From the *Collaborate* tab>Synchronize panel, click 🖥️ (Worksharing Monitor).

  - You can open System Performance to monitor your computer's resources, like hard drive space, memory, and CPU load.

  - The Worksharing Monitor for Autodesk Revit 2024 dialog box needs to remain open while you work in order to receive desktop notifications.

- To specify notification options, click 🔧 (Options).

  - Worksharing Monitor options include General, Central File Access, Editing Request, and Notifications.

Editing Elements in Worksets

There are two different ways to edit elements in worksets.

- **Borrow elements:** If you *borrow* the elements as you make changes, no one has to wait for permission to make modifications. After the interior wall is moved (as shown in Figure 4–54), it will show that you have borrowed the workset that the element is on (as shown in Figure 4–55). This method allows others to modify elements on the same workset without requesting permission.This can speed up the work if you have a fairly small group of people working on the project, especially when there is some overlap between the purposes of the users or when the project has only been divided into a few worksets.

Worksets				
Active workset:				
Interior Level 1 (Not Editable) ⌄		☐ Gray Inactive Workset Graphic		
Name	Editable	Owner	Borrowe	Opened
Exterior	No			Yes
Furniture	No			Yes
Interior Level 1	No		User2	Yes
Plumbing	No			Yes
Shared Levels and Grids	No			Yes
Vertical circulation	No			Yes

Figure 4–54   **Figure 4–55**

Note: Check with your project coordinator to see which method your office uses.

- **Check out a workset:** When you *check out* a specific workset and make it editable, no one else can modify elements in that workset without placing a request to borrow an element.

Borrowing Elements

When you select an element and see the **Make element editable** icon, as shown in Figure 4–56, it means that you have not checked out that particular workset or that you are not currently borrowing the element.

*Note: The **Make element editable** icon needs to be turned on to be visible in the project. To turn this icon on, in the Collaborate tab, expand the Manage Collaboration panel and check the checkbox for **Show Worksharing Make Editable Controls**. If more than one element is selected, the icon will not display unless* (Active Controls) *is activated.*

Figure 4–56

- It is not necessary to click the icon; simply proceed to edit the element.

    - If you modify the element and it enables you to do so, then no one else has that workset checked out and you were given automatic permission to modify this element.

    - If someone else has borrowed the element or checked out the workset to which it belongs, you are prompted to request permission to edit the element.

How To: Check Out Worksets

1. In the *Collaborate* tab>Manage Collaboration panel, click (Worksets).

   Note: You can also open the Worksets dialog box from the Status Bar.

2. In the Worksets dialog box, select **Yes** in the *Editable* column next to the workset name that you want to check out and edit, as shown in Figure 4–57. More than one workset can be checked out and made editable at a time, but ensure that you only check out the ones that you really need.

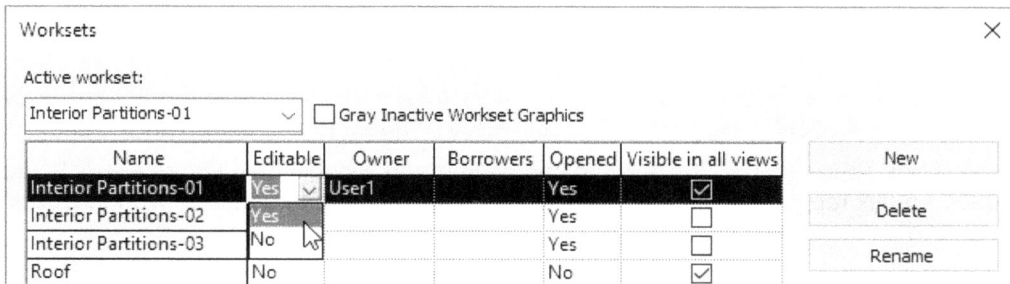

Figure 4–57

3. Select an **Active workset** in the drop-down list. You can also set the active workset from the list in either the Manage Collaboration panel or Status Bar.

4. Click **OK**.

•   When editing elements, you can control which ones can be picked by selecting the **Editable Only** option in the Options Bar, as shown in Figure 4–58. If **Editable Only** is selected, you can only select items that are available in the editable worksets or those which you borrowed. If it is cleared, you can select anything.

Figure 4–58

Permissions to Edit

If you try to edit an element that is owned by someone else, an alert box opens stating that you cannot edit the element without their permission, as shown in Figure 4–59. First, you must request an edit. Second, the owner of the workset either grants or denies the request. If the request is granted, update your local file and you will have control of the element until you relinquish it.

Figure 4–59

How To: Request an Edit

1. When the alert box opens stating that you need to have permission to modify an element (as shown previously in Figure 4–59), click **Place Request** to ask to borrow the element.

2. An alert box opens stating the request has been made, as shown in Figure 4–60. If you expect a quick reply, leave the message in place. If you want to continue working, click **Close** and cancel out of the alert box. The request is still active.

Figure 4–60

How To: Grant or Deny an Editing Request

1. When a user sends an editing request for an element you are currently borrowing or which belongs to a workset that you have checked out (editable), an Editing Request Received alert displays, as shown in Figure 4–61.

Figure 4–61

Note: The Editing Request alert may display off screen due to your screen resolution or having multiple monitors. Search "editing request notification" on Autodesk's Revit knowledge base for information on how to resolve this issue.

- Alternatively, you can access the editing requests you receive from the Status Bar or from the *Collaborate* tab>Communicate panel>**Editing Requests**. The **Editing Request** icon in the Status Bar will display a number next to it once an editing request has been placed, as shown in Figure 4–62.

Before an editing request is placed   *After an editing request is placed*

Figure 4–62

2. In the Editing Request Received dialog box, click **Show** to zoom in to the element requested, **Grant** to allow the other user to modify the element, or **Deny** to stop the other user from modifying the element.

3. If you do not respond right away to the editing request, you can always access it again. In the *Collaborate* tab>Synchronize panel, click (Editing Requests (no requests pending)) or in the Status Bar, click (Editing Requests (requests pending)). The information in the Status Bar includes the number of requests outstanding, as shown in Figure 4–63.

Figure 4–63

4. In the Editing Requests dialog box, select the pending request by clicking on the date, as shown in Figure 4–64.

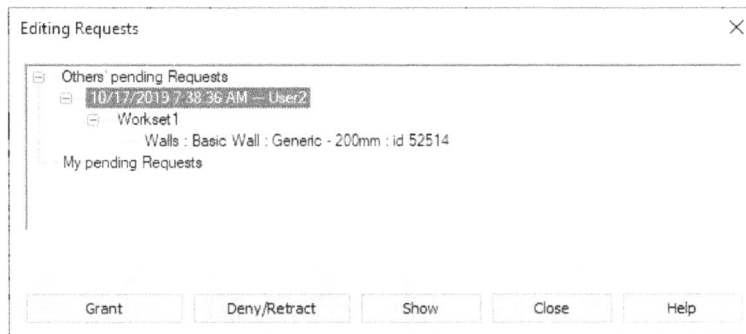

Figure 4–64

- When you select the editing request date, the elements included in the request are highlighted in the project. Click **Show** to zoom in on the elements, if needed.

5. Click **Grant** to enable the other user to make the changes or **Deny/Retract** to deny the request. (The original user can also retract the request with this button.) You can also grant the request by saving the entire workset back to the central model and relinquishing the items.

Applying an Editing Request

When an editing request is granted or denied, a confirmation alert box opens in the program of the user who requested it, as shown for a granted request in Figure 4–65. Close the alert box.

Figure 4–65

Note: Once a request is granted, you can make modifications to the element without having to request to edit the feature, although the icon still displays.

- If the requesting user canceled out of the Editing Request Placed dialog box, when they are notified that they have permission, they can click (Reload Latest) or type **RL** to make the ownership modification.

- If the Error dialog box is still open when the request is granted, the Editing Request Placed dialog box displays that the request has been granted, as shown on in Figure 4–66. Click **Close** and the element is modified.

Note: An additional note "Reload Latest is required to edit the elements" might display in the dialog box depending on what the other user did with the borrowed elements.

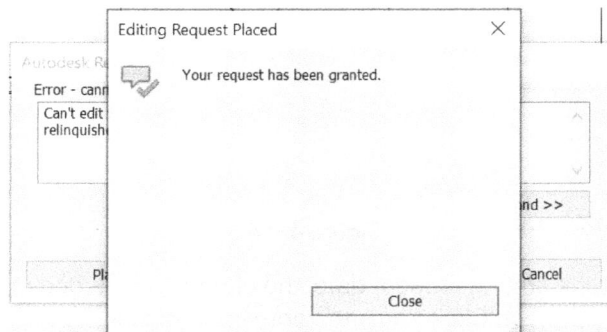

Figure 4–66

- If the request has been denied (as shown in Figure 4–67), click **Close**. The element remains as is.

Figure 4–67

Editing Request Frequency

To control the frequency of updates to editing requests (and worksharing display modes), in the Options dialog box, in the *General* tab, move the slider bar between *Less Frequent* and *More Frequent*, as shown in Figure 4–68.

Figure 4–68

- If the bar is moved to the far side of *Less Frequent*, it changes to manual and updates only when you borrow elements or synchronize with the central model. This can improve the performance of the program but also causes the other user to wait until you receive the request.

Relinquishing Worksets

After you have been working with borrowed elements or have checked out worksets, you should return them to the central model when you are finished. In the Quick Access Toolbar or

Collaborate tab>Synchronize panel, click ⬚ (Synchronize and Modify Settings). The Synchronize with Central dialog box displays, as shown in Figure 4–69. In this dialog box, select the worksets and/or borrowed elements you want to relinquish. Only those which you have ownership of are available.

Figure 4–69

Synchronize with Central Options

- The **Borrowed Elements** option will be selected by default. This relinquishes any elements you borrowed from another workset.

- Select the **Save Local File before and after synchronizing with central** option to save extra steps.

- Periodically, use the **Compact Central Model (slow)** option when you save to the central model. This reduces the file size, but also increases the time required to save.

  Note: Adding comments at key points and for significant changes in the project is useful in case the project backup needs to be restored in the future.

- You can add comments to the central model for others to see. To view the comments, in the

  Collaborate tab>Synchronize panel, click ⬚ (Show History) and select the central model whose history you want to view. The History dialog box displays with the *Date/Time Stamp*, *Modified by*, and *Comments* columns populated with information, as shown in Figure 4–70.

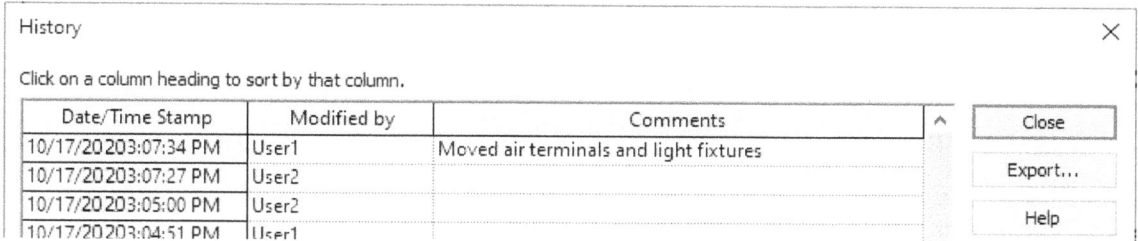

Date/Time Stamp	Modified by	Comments	^	Close
10/17/2020 3:07:34 PM	User1	Moved air terminals and light fixtures		Export...
10/17/2020 3:07:27 PM	User2			
10/17/2020 3:05:00 PM	User2			Help
10/17/2020 3:04:51 PM	User1			

History

Click on a column heading to sort by that column.

Figure 4–70

4.7 Visibility and Display Options with Worksharing

While using worksets, there are certain display tools to help you as you work. Worksets can be toggled off and on in the Visibility/Graphic Overrides dialog box. You can use the Worksharing Display settings to graphically differentiate by color, such as indicating the Owners of different elements or the elements that need to be updated.

Controlling Workset Visibility

Not all worksets need to be visible in every view. For example, the exterior shell of a building should display in most views, but interior walls or the site features only need to be displayed in related views. The default workset visibility is controlled when the workset is first created, but can be managed in the Visibility/Graphic Overrides dialog box, as shown in Figure 4–71.

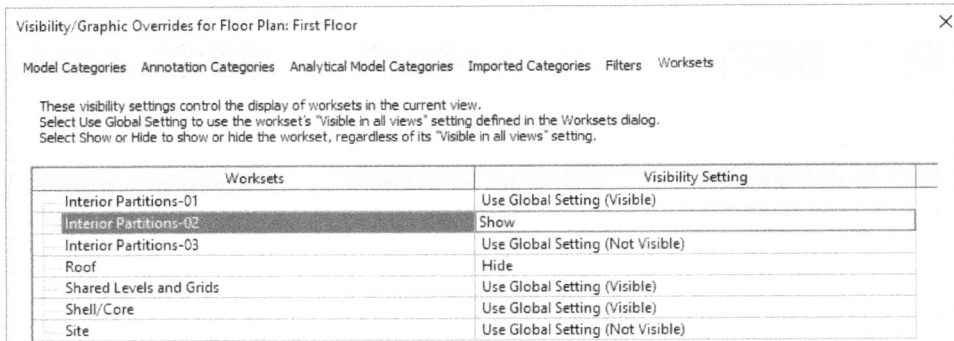

Visibility/Graphic Overrides for Floor Plan: First Floor   ×

Model Categories   Annotation Categories   Analytical Model Categories   Imported Categories   Filters   Worksets

These visibility settings control the display of worksets in the current view.
Select Use Global Setting to use the workset's "Visible in all views" setting defined in the Worksets dialog.
Select Show or Hide to show or hide the workset, regardless of its "Visible in all views" setting.

Worksets	Visibility Setting
Interior Partitions-01	Use Global Setting (Visible)
Interior Partitions-02	Show
Interior Partitions-03	Use Global Setting (Not Visible)
Roof	Hide
Shared Levels and Grids	Use Global Setting (Visible)
Shell/Core	Use Global Setting (Visible)
Site	Use Global Setting (Not Visible)

Figure 4–71

How To: Change the Visibility of Worksets

Note: Limiting the number of worksets speeds up the process of opening and saving the file. It is recommended that you close a workset that is not required rather than change its visibility.

1. Type **VV** or **VG** to open the Visibility/Graphic Overrides dialog box.
2. Select the *Worksets* tab. Modify the *Visibility Setting* for each workset, as required. Changing the setting to **Show** or **Hide** only impacts the current view.
3. Click **OK** to close the dialog box.

- Worksets marked with an asterisk (*) have not been opened in this session of Revit and are therefore not visible in any view.

- Closing worksets toggles off element visibility in all views. It also saves more computer memory than just toggling off the display of worksets.

- The *Worksets* tab in the Visibility/Graphic Overrides dialog box is only available when worksets have been enabled.

- These overrides can also be set up in a view template.

Worksharing Display Options

A handy way to view the status of elements in worksharing is to set the Worksharing Display. For example, when you set the Worksharing Display to **Worksets**, as shown in Figure 4–72, the elements in each workset are highlighted in a different color.

Figure 4–72

There are several types of worksharing displays: **Checkout Status**, **Owners**, **Model Updates**, and **Worksets**. You can access them in the Status Bar, as shown in Figure 4–73.

Figure 4–73

- As you hover the cursor over elements in a view with a worksharing display selected, information about the element displays, depending on the type you selected (as shown in Figure 4–74).

  Note: *Toggling on Gray Inactive Worksets while using Worksharing Display might change the display status of elements in two tones of the same color.*

Figure 4–74

- You can modify the colors in the Worksharing Display Settings dialog box, as well as select which items you want to display, as shown in Figure 4–75.

Figure 4–75

4.8 Worksharing and Linked Models

Note: *All images in the upcoming sections refer to users as "User1" or "User2". In your working environment, you will see your unique Revit username in these dialog boxes.*

When you are working in a workshared project, each linked model should be in a separate workset. For example, before linking in a structural model, specify and set the appropriate workset, as shown in Figure 4–76. When you open a local file, you can specify which worksets you want to display, as shown in Figure 4–77.

Figure 4–76

Figure 4–77

The same is true if you are linking in a model that has been workshared. You can control which worksets are open and which worksets display. In this case, the worksets from the linked model are not available for modification or use in the host project (which might have its own worksets).

• Remember that limiting the number of worksets you open and display speeds up the process of opening and saving the file. It is recommended that you close a workset that is not required rather than change its visibility. When working with linked files, you can also close them, as shown in Figure 4–78.

Worksets

Active workset:

| Structural link | ⌄ | ☐ Gray Inactive Workset Graphics |

Name	Editable	Owner	Borrowe	Opened	Visible in all views
Exterior Shell	Yes	User1		Yes	☑
HVAC link	Yes	User1		No	☐
Plumbing link	Yes	User1		No	☐
Shared Levels and Grids	Yes	User1		Yes	☑
Structural link	Yes	User1		Yes	☑

Figure 4–78

Managing Links in Local Files

When you open a local file that includes linked models set up in separate worksets, you can choose to unload each link for just yourself or for all users. In the Manage Links dialog box, as shown in Figure 4–79, select the link and in the *Unload* area, select either **For all users** or **For me**.

Figure 4–79

- If you unload for all users, the link will still be available but will be unloaded by default anytime someone else opens a local file. You will need to place a request to reload it if the original person that unloaded the link has not relinquished it.

- If you unload a link just for yourself, this action is remembered when you synchronize with the central model. If you want to reload the link, select it and click **Clear my override**.

Managing Worksets in Linked Models

Linked models that include worksets can be managed at two levels. You can load and unload the entire link or you can open and close the individual worksets in the linked model. For example, you might want the Site workset turned on in some views but not in others, as shown in Figure 4–80.

- Worksets can also be set as visible in some views and not visible in other views.

Figure 4–80

How To: Open and Close Worksets in a Linked Model

1. Open the Manage Links dialog box.

2. In the Manage Links dialog box, select the link that includes worksets, as shown in Figure 4–81, and click **Manage Worksets**.

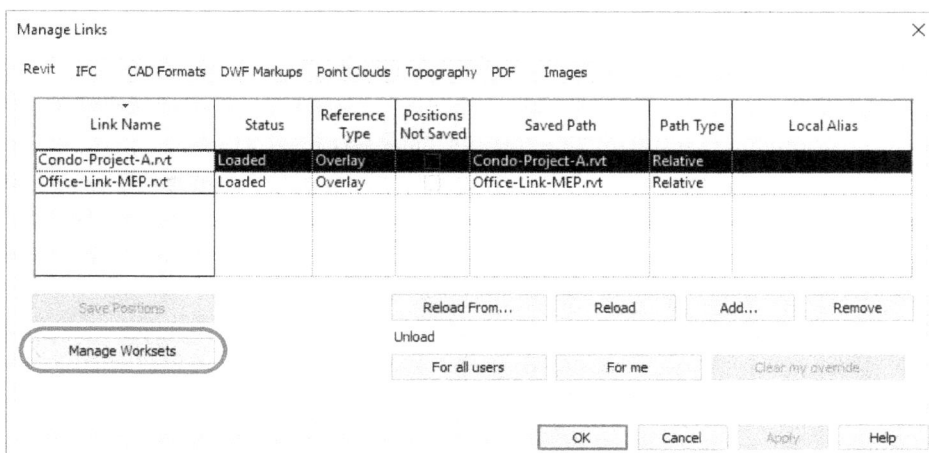

Figure 4–81

- The **Manage Worksets** button will be grayed out if there are no worksets associated with a link.

3. In the Manage Worksets for Link dialog box, select the workset(s) you want to close and click **Close**, or select the workset(s) you want to open and click **Open**. For example, in Figure 4–82, the linked Roof and Site worksets have been closed.

Figure 4–82

4. Click **Reload** and the link displays only the worksets that are opened.

How To: Change the Visibility of Worksets in a Linked Model

1. Type **VV** to open the Visibility/Graphic Overrides dialog box.

2. Click on the *Revit Links* tab. This tab only displays if there are links in the project.

3. In the *Display Settings* column, beside the link, click **<By Host View>**.

4. In the RVT Link Display Settings dialog box, in the *Basics* tab, select **Custom**, as shown in Figure 4–83.

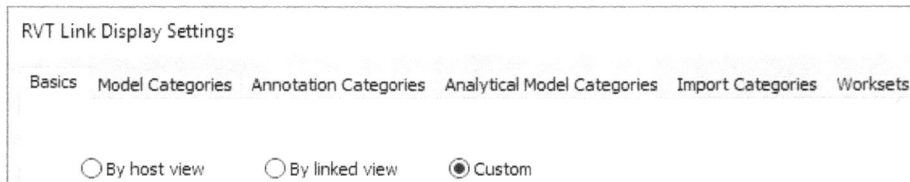

Figure 4–83

5. Select the *Worksets* tab and set the *Worksets* to **<Custom>**. This enables you to modify the visibility of individual worksets as needed. For example, in Figure 4–84, the **Interior Partitions** worksets are cleared, indicating that they are not visible in the current view.

- Worksets that display with **(Closed)*** do not display in any view.

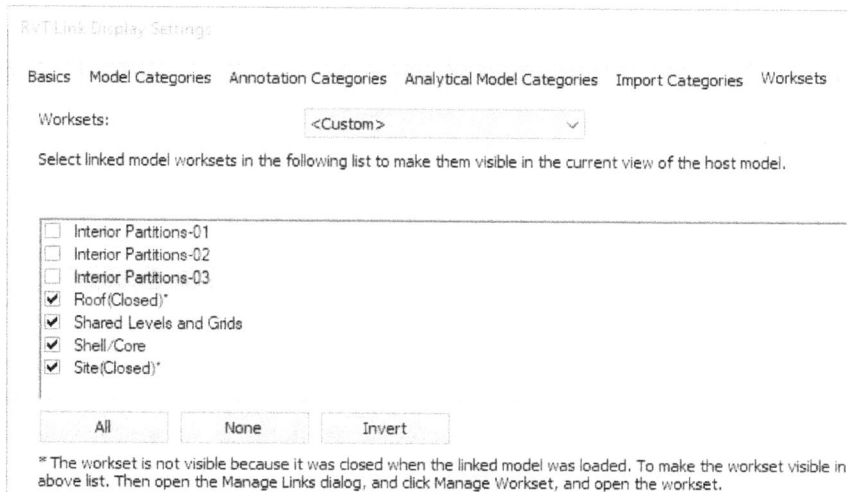

Figure 4–84

6. Click **OK** to close the dialog boxes.

Practice 4d
Work in a Workshared Project - Architectural

Practice Objectives

- Work in pairs to simulate a worksharing environment.
- Update an existing central model for use in the practice.
- Create a local file of the central model from each copy of the software.

In this practice, you will need to work in pairs to simulate a worksharing environment. On your individual machines, User1 and User2 will each create a local file and select specific worksets to open in each project, as shown in Figure 4–85. One user within the pair will create the central model.

> 💡 **NOTE: Special Instructions for Instructors and Students**
>
> - Instructors: You will need to create a shared network folder for students to work in pairs to simulate the work environment.
> - Students: If this is self-paced training and you are not able to work in pairs or save a central model to a shared network location, you can watch the **Work in a Workshared Project-Architectural.mp4** video, located in the practice files *Videos* folder, for a demonstration of the tasks in this practice.

"User1" and "User2" are referenced throughout the practice but you will see your unique Revit username instead.

Worksets

Active workset:

| Interior Partitions-01 | ∨ | ☐ Gray Inactive Workset Graphics |

Name	Editable	Owner	Borrowers	Opened	Visible in all v
Interior Partitions-01	Yes	User1		Yes	☑
Interior Partitions-02	No			Yes	☐
Interior Partitions-03	No			Yes	☐
Roof	No			No	☑
Shared Levels and Grids	No			Yes	☑
Shell/Core	No			Yes	☑
Site	No			No	☐

Figure 4–85

This practice uses a project that has been subdivided into worksets. To simulate a worksharing environment, work in groups of two. To keep the practices simple, the terms "User1" and "User2" will be used to indicate which user is to do certain tasks.

- **User1** updates the central model and focuses on the interiors of the condo units.

- **User2** focuses on the exterior and core.

Task 1: Save the central model to the shared folder location.

1. **User1**, verify no projects are open. On the Home screen, in the *MODELS* section, click **Open...**. In the practice files *Architectural* folder, open **Condo-Project-A-M.rvt**.

2. Alert boxes about a **Copied Central Model** and/or **Cannot Find Central Model** might display. Read and then close the alert boxes.

    - A central model needs to be repathed if it has been relocated. You will typically not have to do this in a work environment, but will need to do it for this practice to work.

3. In the *File* tab, expand 🖫 (Save As) and click 🗐 (Project).

4. In the Save As dialog box, click **Options...**.

5. In the File Save Options dialog box, select **Make this a Central Model after save** and then click **OK**.

6. Verify that the name is still set to **Condo-Project-A-M.rvt**, navigate to the shared network folder location, and click **Save**.

    - If the Workset File Already Exists dialog box displays, click **Yes** to replace the existing file.

7. Close the project.

Task 2: Create the local file for User1.

1. **User1** continues working within Revit.

2. On the Home screen, in the *MODELS* section, click **Open...**. Navigate to the shared network folder location and select **Condo-Project-A-M.rvt**.

3. Verify that **Create New Local** is selected, as shown in Figure 4–86, and click **Open**.

File name:	Condo-Project-A-M.rvt
Files of type:	All Supported Files (*.rvt, *.rfa, *.adsk, *.rte)

Worksharing

☐ Audit   ☐ Detach from Central   ☑ Create New Local   Open ▼   Cancel

Figure 4–86

4. The file opens and displays the name **Condo-Project-A-M_User1.rvt** at the top of the interface.

   - Note what the file name is at the top of your Revit user interface. It should have the file name with your unique username at the end.

5. In the *Collaborate* tab>Manage Collaboration panel or in the Status Bar, click

   (Worksets).

6. In the Worksets dialog box, do the following, as shown in Figure 4–87:

   - Verify the *Active workset* is **Interior Partitions-01**.

   - In the list of worksets, select **Interior Partitions-01**, select **Editable** to set the *Editable* column to **Yes**, and verify that **Visible in all views** is checked.

   - Select the worksets **Roof** and **Site**. Click **Close** so that the worksets are not open in this session.

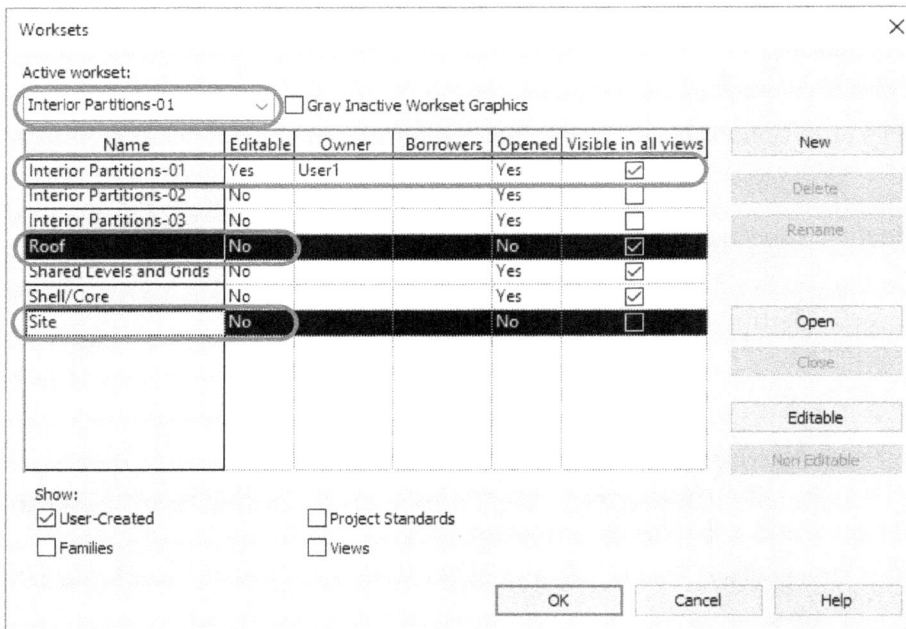

Figure 4–87

7. Click **OK** to finish.

8. In the Quick Access Toolbar, click (Save) to save the local file.

Task 3: Create the local file for User2.

1. **User2**, verify no projects are open. On the Home screen, in the *MODELS* section, click **Open...**.

2. Navigate to the shared network folder location and select the file **Condo-Project-A-M.rvt**. Verify that **Create New Local** is selected. Click the arrow next to **Open** and select **Specify...** in the drop-down list, as shown in Figure 4–88.

Figure 4–88

3. Click **Open** to open the project.

4. In the Opening Worksets dialog box, select the three **Interior Partitions** worksets and click **Close** so that these worksets are not opened in this session, as shown in Figure 4–89.

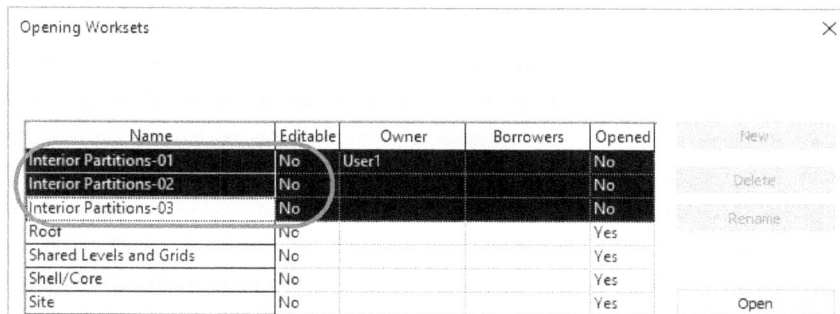

Figure 4–89

5. Click **OK** to finish.

   Note: The file name at the top of your Revit user interface should have your unique username at the end.

6. In the Quick Access Toolbar, click 💾 (Save) to save the local file. Keep the file open.

Task 4: Add and modify elements in worksets.

1. **User1,** in your local file for Condo-Project-A-M, verify that you are in the **Floor Plans: First Floor** view.

2. Zoom in on Unit 1C and a wall using the interior wall type **Basic Wall: Generic - 200mm** with the *Top Constraint* set to **Second Floor**. Draw the wall so that it butts up against an existing window, as shown in Figure 4–90. A warning displays, noting that the insert conflicts with the joined wall.

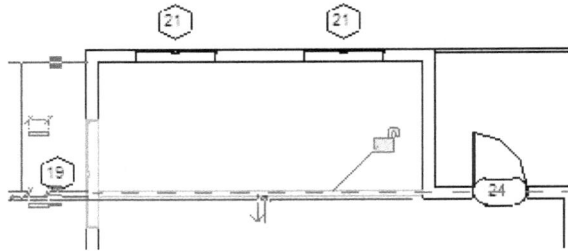

Figure 4–90

3. Close the warning.

4. Click **Modify**.

5. Move the window so it does not conflict with the wall.

6. Open the Worksets dialog box. **User1** will be noted as the *Owner* of the **Interior Partitions-01** workset and a *Borrower* of the **Shell/Core** workset, as shown in Figure 4–91.

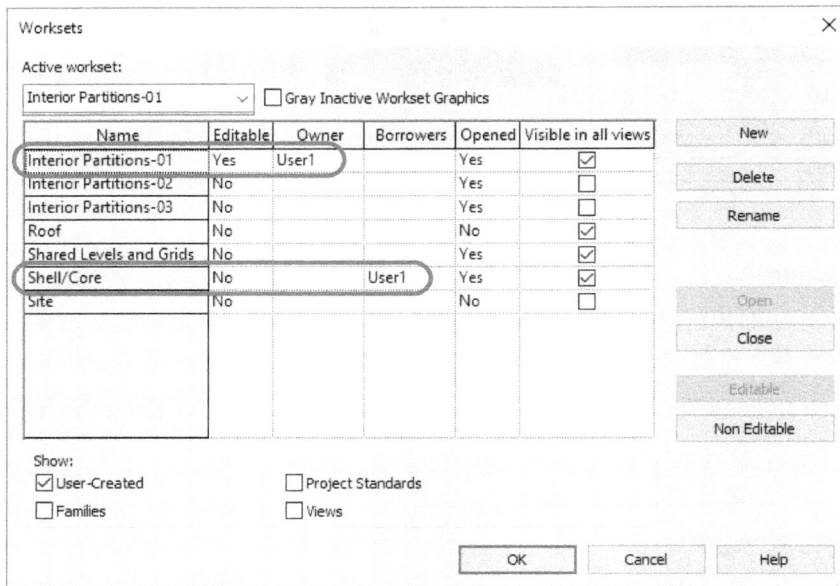

Figure 4–91

7. Click **OK** to close the dialog box.

8. In the *Collaborate* tab>Synchronize panel or in the Quick Access Toolbar, click

    (Synchronize and Modify Settings) to open the Synchronize with Central dialog box. The **Borrowed Elements** option should be selected. Add a comment about moving the window and select the **Save Local File before and after synchronizing with central** option, as shown in Figure 4–92. (Your central model location may differ from that in the figure.)

Figure 4–92

9. Click **OK**.

Task 5: Check out a workset.

1. **User2**, verify you are in the **Floor Plans: First Floor** view. None of the changes show in the local file.

2. In the *Collaborate* tab>Synchronize panel, click (Reload Latest), or type **RL**. The window location changes but you might not see the new walls if that workset is not open and visible.

3. Click (Worksets) to open the dialog box.

4. In the *Visible in all views* column, verify that **Interior Partitions-01** is checked and click **Open**.

5. Select **Shell/Core** and click **Editable**. The *Owner* should display as **User 2**, as shown in Figure 4–93.

Name	Editable	Owner	Borrowers	Opened	Visible in all views
Interior Partitions-01	No	User1		Yes	☑
Interior Partitions-02	No			Yes	☐
Interior Partitions-03	No			Yes	☐
Roof	No			Yes	☑
Shared Levels and Grids	No			Yes	☑
Shell/Core	Yes	User2		Yes	☑
Site	No			Yes	☐

Active workset: Shell/Core   ☐ Gray Inactive Workset Graphics

Figure 4–93

6. Click **OK** to close the dialog box.

7. Move door number 5 in Unit 1A down in the wall so that it is no longer opposite to door number 6.

8. In the Quick Access Toolbar, click 💾 (Save) to save the local file.

9. **User1**, type **RL** (Reload Latest). There are no new changes to load, as shown in Figure 4–94, because User2 has not saved back to the central model. Close the dialog box.

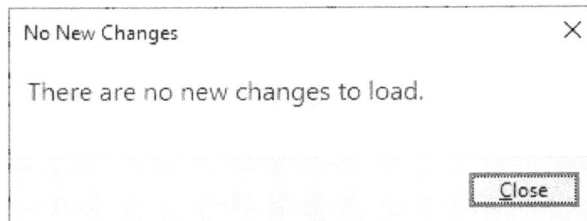

No New Changes   ×

There are no new changes to load.

Close

Figure 4–94

10. **User2** will click 🧊 (Synchronize Now). This saves the changes to the central model without relinquishing the Shell/Core workset.

Task 6: Request permission to edit.

1. **User1**, type **RL** (Reload Latest) again. This time, the door moves in response to the change made in the central model.

2. Try to move the door back where it was. This time, an error message displays that cannot be ignored, as shown in Figure 4–95. **User2** has made the Shell/Core workset editable. Therefore, other users cannot edit elements in it without permission.

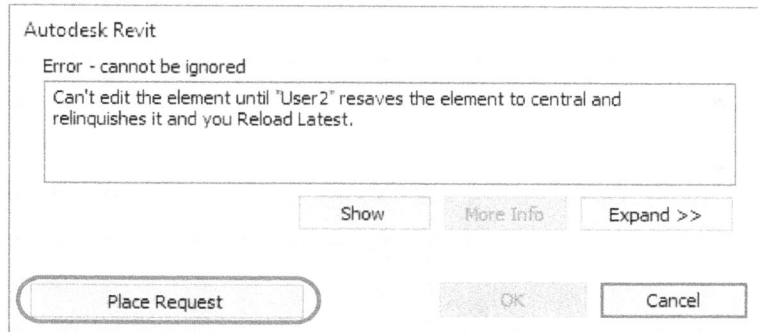

Autodesk Revit

Error - cannot be ignored

Can't edit the element until "User2" resaves the element to central and relinquishes it and you Reload Latest.

| Show | More Info | Expand >> |

| Place Request | OK | Cancel |

Figure 4–95

3. Click **Place Request**. The Editing Request Placed dialog box opens. Leave the dialog boxes opened, as shown in Figure 4–96.

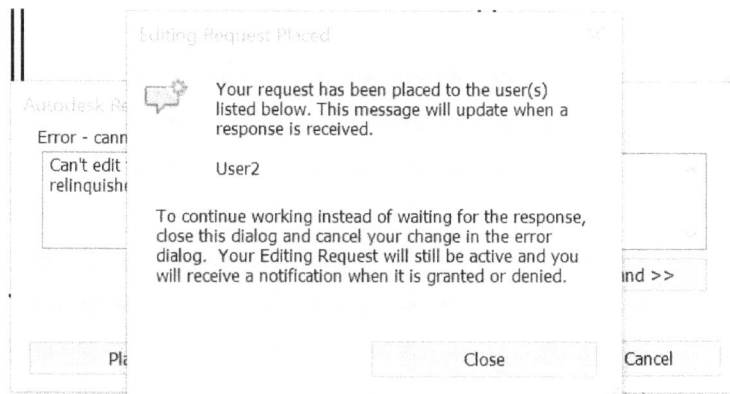

Editing Request Placed

Your request has been placed to the user(s) listed below. This message will update when a response is received.

User2

To continue working instead of waiting for the response, close this dialog and cancel your change in the error dialog. Your Editing Request will still be active and you will receive a notification when it is granted or denied.

Close

Figure 4–96

4. **User2** now has a number **1** next to the **Editing Request** icon in the Status Bar, as shown in Figure 4–97. Click (Editing Request) to open the Editing Requests dialog box.

Shell/Core

Figure 4–97

- Alternatively, an Editing Request Received alert should display that can be used to access the Editing Requests dialog box, but it may be off screen.

5. Expand the nodes to view more details about the request, as shown in Figure 4–98. Move the dialog box out of the way, if needed, to see the door is highlighted.

Figure 4–98

6. Select the first node under **Others' pending Requests**, as shown above in Figure 4–98, and click **Grant** to give the other user permission to modify the placement of this door. By doing this, you enable the other user full control over this one element in the workset.

7. **User1** will get an Editing Request Placed dialog box with a *Your request has been granted* message, as shown in Figure 4–99.

Figure 4–99

8. Close the Editing Request Placed dialog box. Because your request was granted, the door moves.

9. Move the door again to exactly where you want it. This time, you are not prompted to ask to move the door because you are still borrowing it.

10. Try to move another door. You do not have permission to move this door. Click **Cancel** rather than place the request. The door returns to its original location.

Task 7: View information about the worksets.

1. **User1,** in the View Control Bar, expand the Worksharing Display and click ⬡ (Owners). Different colors highlight the elements and their respective owners. Hover the cursor over one of the walls to display information about the owner, as shown in Figure 4–100.

Figure 4–100

*   The color on your display might be different.

2. Zoom out so you can see the full floor plan.

3. Click ⬡ (Synchronize and Modify Settings) and relinquish **User-created Worksets** and **Borrowed Elements.**

4. The new interior walls once displayed as owned by **User1** are now not in color and the door that was borrowed returns to the original owner **User2**.

5. Toggle the Worksharing Display off.

6. Save the local file.

7. **User2**, click ⬡ (Synchronize Now) without relinquishing **User-created Worksets**. The door moves to the location where **User1** moved it. When you save to the central model, it also reloads the latest changes.

8. Close the project. When the Editable Elements dialog box opens, as shown in Figure 4–101, click **Relinquish elements and worksets**.

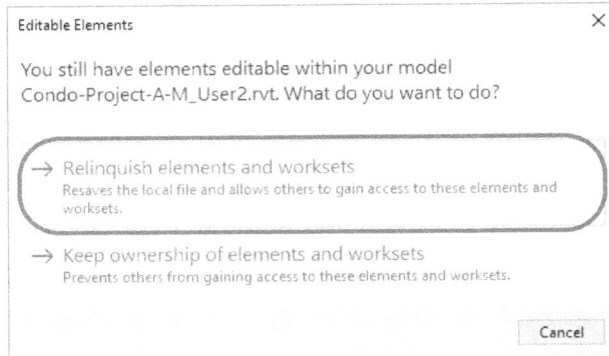

Figure 4–101

9. **User1**, close the project and synchronize with central.

End of practice

Practice 4e
Work in a Workshared Project - Structural

Practice Objectives

- Work in pairs to simulate a worksharing environment.
- Update an existing central model for use in the practice.
- Create a local file of the central model from each copy of the software.

In this practice, you will need to work in pairs to simulate a worksharing environment. On your individual machines, User1 and User2 will each create a local file and select specific worksets to open in each project, as shown in Figure 4–102. One user within the pair will create the central model.

💡 NOTE: Special Instructions for Instructors and Students

- Instructors: You will need to create a shared network folder for students to work in pairs to simulate the work environment.
- Students: If this is self-paced training and you are not able to work in pairs or save a central model to a shared network location, you can watch the **Work in a Workshared Project-Architectural.mp4** video, located in the practice files *Videos* folder, for a demonstration of the tasks in the Architectural practice.

"User1" and "User2" are referenced throughout the practice but you will see your unique Revit username instead.

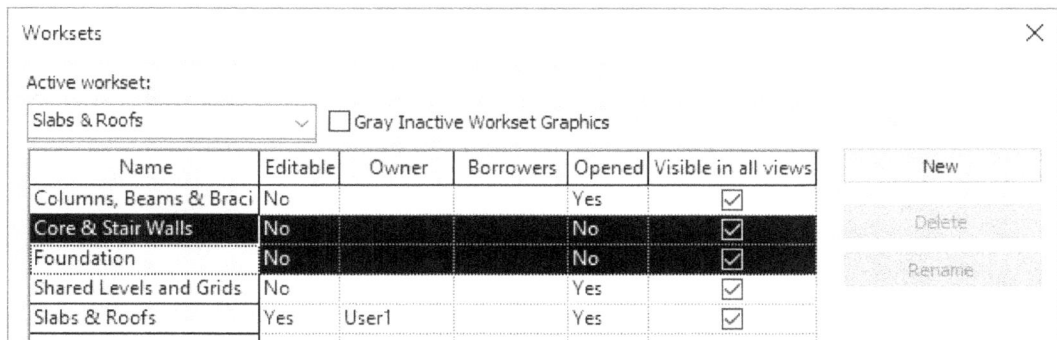

Name	Editable	Owner	Borrowers	Opened	Visible in all views
Columns, Beams & Braci	No			Yes	☑
Core & Stair Walls	No			No	☑
Foundation	No			No	☑
Shared Levels and Grids	No			Yes	☑
Slabs & Roofs	Yes	User1		Yes	☑

Active workset: Slabs & Roofs

Figure 4–102

This practice uses a project that has been subdivided into worksets. To simulate a worksharing environment, work in groups of two. To keep the practices simple, the terms "User1" and "User2" will be used to indicate which user is to do certain tasks.

- **User1** updates the central model and focuses on the floor slabs.

- **User2** focuses on the core and stair walls.

Task 1: Open and save the central model to the shared folder location.

1. **User1**, verify no projects are open. On the Home screen, in the *MODELS* section, click **Open...**. In the practice files *Structural* folder, open **Syracuse-Suites-S-M.rvt**.

2. Alert boxes about a **Copied Central Model** and/or **Cannot Find Central Model** might display. Read and then close the alert boxes.

   - A central model needs to be repathed if it has been relocated. You will typically not have to do this in a work environment, but will need to do it for this practice to work.

3. In the *File* tab, expand 🖫 (Save As) and click 🖼 (Project).

4. In the Save As dialog box, click **Options...**.

5. In the File Save Options dialog box, select **Make this a Central Model after save** and then click **OK**.

6. Verify that the name is still set to **Syracuse-Suites-S-M.rvt**, navigate to the shared network folder location, and click **Save**.

   - If the Workset File Already Exists dialog box displays, click **Yes** to replace the existing file.

7. Close the project.

Task 2: Create the local file for User1.

1. **User1** continues working within Revit.

2. On the Home screen, in the *MODELS* section, click **Open...**. Navigate to the shared network folder location and select **Syracuse-Suites-S-M.rvt**.

3. Verify that **Create New Local** is selected and click **Open**. A file with the name **Syracuse-Suites-S-M_User1.rvt** is opened.

   - Note what the file name is at the top of your Revit user interface. It should have the file name with your unique username at the end.

4. In the *Collaborate* tab>Manage Collaboration panel or in the Status Bar, click 🏗 (Worksets).

5. In the Worksets dialog box, make **Slabs & Roofs** the Active workset. Select **Editable** to set the *Editable* column to **Yes** and verify that **Visible in all views** is checked. Select the **Core & Stair Walls** and **Foundation** worksets. Click **Close** so the worksets are not open in this session, as shown in Figure 4–103.

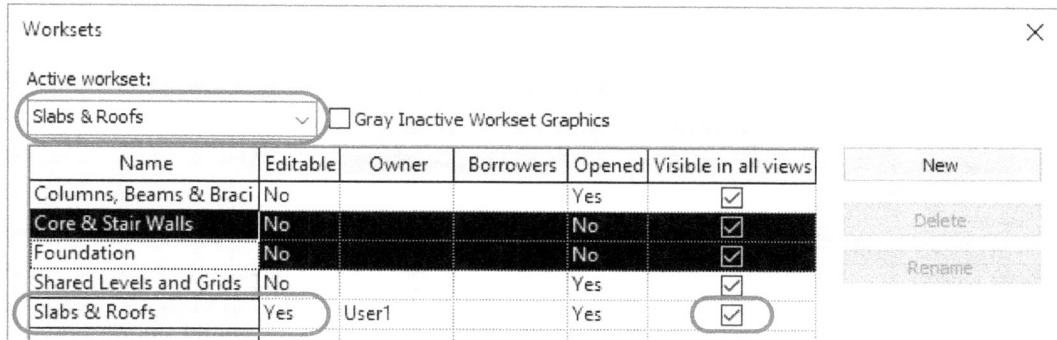

Figure 4–103

6. Click **OK** to finish.

7. In the Quick Access Toolbar, click 💾 (Save) to save the local file.

Task 3: Create the local file for User2.

1. **User2**, on the Home screen, in the *MODELS* section, click **Open...**. Navigate to the shared network folder location and select **Syracuse-Suites-S-M.rvt**. Verify that **Create New Local** is selected.

2. Click the arrow next to **Open**, and select **Specify...** in the drop-down list, as shown in Figure 4–104.

Figure 4–104

3. Click **Open** to open the project.

4. In the Opening Worksets dialog box, select the **Columns, Beams & Bracing** and **Slabs & Roofs** worksets and click **Close** so these worksets are not opened in this session, as shown in Figure 4–105.

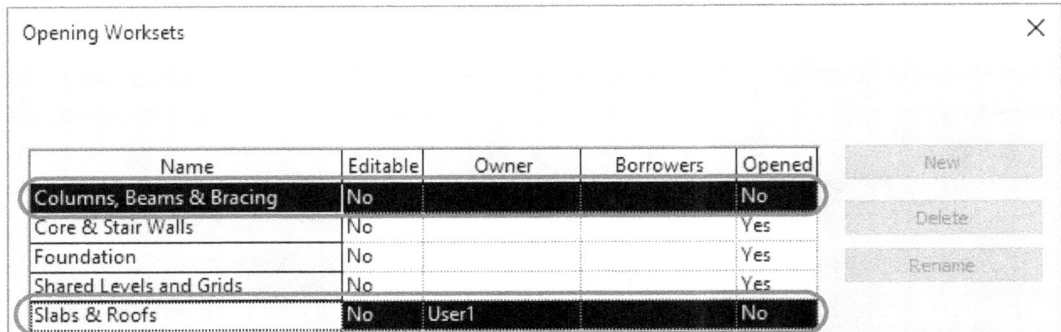

Name	Editable	Owner	Borrowers	Opened
Columns, Beams & Bracing	No			No
Core & Stair Walls	No			Yes
Foundation	No			Yes
Shared Levels and Grids	No			Yes
Slabs & Roofs	No	User1		No

Figure 4–105

5. Click **OK** to finish.

    Note: The file name at the top of your Revit user interface should have your unique username at the end.

6. Save the local file.

Task 4: Add and modify elements in worksets.

1. **User1**, in your local file for Syracuse-Suites-S-M, verify the **Structural Plans: 1ST FLOOR** view is the current view.

2. Zoom in on the beam system between grid lines 6 and 7 and C and D. Stay far enough out so that you can see the edge of the building, as shown in Figure 4–106. Do not select the beam system.

Figure 4–106

3. Select the second beam from the top and type **UP** to unpin it from the beam system. Move it up so that the distance between the beams is larger, as shown in Figure 4–107.

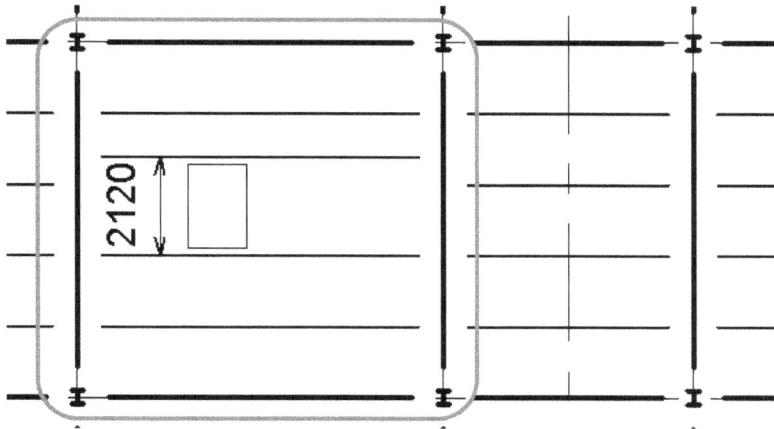

Figure 4–107

4. Hover the cursor over the edge of the building and press <Tab> until the floor is highlighted. Select the floor.

5. In the *Modify | Floors* tab>Mode panel, click (Edit Boundary).

6. In the Draw panel, click (Boundary Line) and draw a rectangle, as shown in Figure 4–108, to add a new opening in the floor. Move the opening inside the framing system between two beams, as shown in Figure 4–108. An exact location is not required for this practice.

Figure 4–108

7. Click (Finish Edit Mode).

8. Click **Modify**.

9. In the *Collaborate* tab>Manage Collaboration panel, in the Active Workset drop-down list, select the **Columns, Beams & Bracing** workset to make it the active workset. It should be listed as **(Not Editable)**.

10. In the *Structure* tab>Structure panel, click ✏️ (Beam).

11. In the Type Selector, verify that the selected beam is **UB-Universal Beam: 305x165x40UB**. In the Options Bar, set the *Structural Usage* to **Joist** and verify the **Chain** option is not checked, as shown in Figure 4–109.

Structural Usage: Joist ☐3D Snapping ☐Chain

Figure 4–109

12. Add two beams to frame the new opening on the unsupported sides, as shown in Figure 4–110.

Columns, Beams & Bracing : Structural Framing : UB-Universal Beam : 305x165x40UB

Figure 4–110

13. Click **Modify** to end the Beam command.

14. In the *Collaborate* tab>Manage Collaboration panel or in the Status Bar, click 🪟 (Worksets).

15. In the Worksets dialog box, **User1** is noted as the *Owner* of the **Slabs & Roofs** workset and as a *Borrower* of **Columns, Beams & Bracing**, as shown in Figure 4–111.

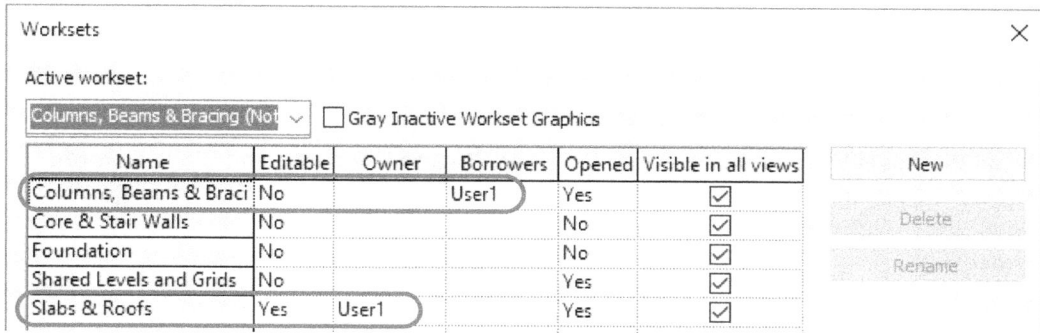

Figure 4–111

16. Close the dialog box.

17. In the Quick Access Toolbar, click (Synchronize and Modify Settings).

18. In the Synchronize with Central dialog box, the **Borrowed Elements** option should be selected and **User-Created Worksets** should be unchecked. Add a comment about adding an opening to the first floor slab and verify that the **Save Local File before and after synchronizing with central** option is selected, as shown in Figure 4–112.

Figure 4–112

19. Click **OK** to finish synchronizing.

Task 5: Check out a workset.

1. **User2**, in the local Syracuse-Suites-S-M file, open the **Structural Plans: 1ST FLOOR** view if it is not already open. None of the changes display in the local file yet.

2. In the Status Bar, click 🗝 (Worksets).

3. In the Worksets dialog box, open the **Columns, Beams & Bracing** and **Slabs & Roofs** worksets by setting the *Opened* column to **Yes**, as shown in Figure 4–113. Click **OK**.

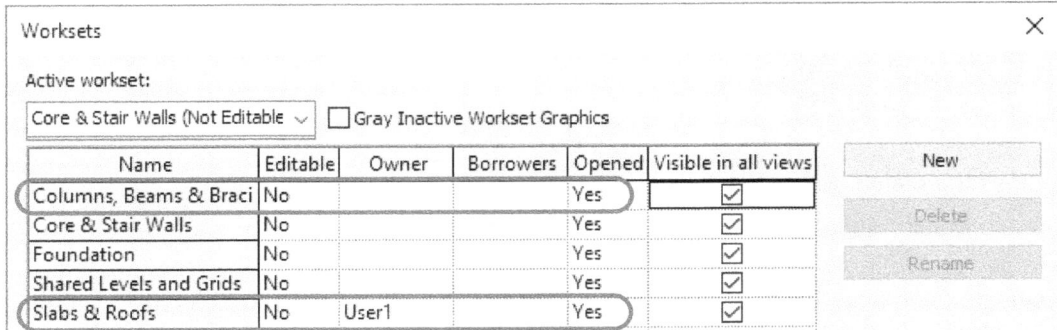

Name	Editable	Owner	Borrowers	Opened	Visible in all views
Columns, Beams & Braci	No			Yes	☑
Core & Stair Walls	No			Yes	☑
Foundation	No			Yes	☑
Shared Levels and Grids	No			Yes	☑
Slabs & Roofs	No	User1		Yes	☑

Figure 4–113

4. In the **Structural Plans: 1ST FLOOR** view, you can now see the beams and other elements, but the changes are still not displayed.

5. In the *Collaborate* tab>Synchronize panel, click 🗝 (Reload Latest) or type **RL**. The new opening and joists display.

6. Open the Worksets dialog box.

7. In the Worksets dialog box, select **Core & Stair Walls** in the list of worksets and make it **Editable**. The *Owner* should change to **User2**, as shown in Figure 4–114.

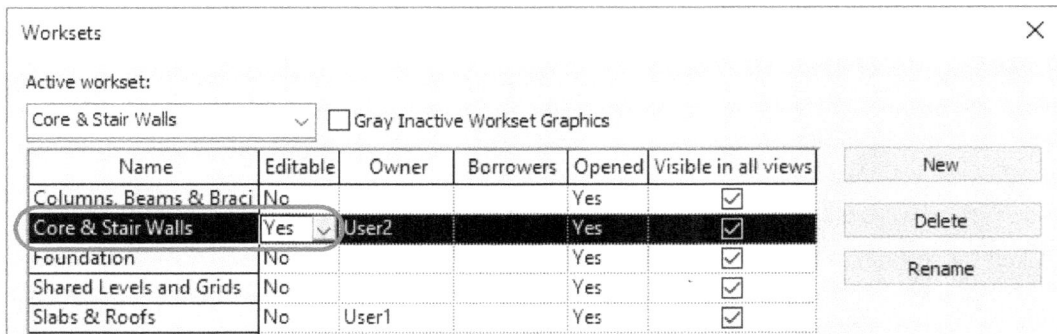

Name	Editable	Owner	Borrowers	Opened	Visible in all views
Columns, Beams & Braci	No			Yes	☑
Core & Stair Walls	Yes	User2		Yes	☑
Foundation	No			Yes	☑
Shared Levels and Grids	No			Yes	☑
Slabs & Roofs	No	User1		Yes	☑

Figure 4–114

8. Click **OK**. Click **Yes** in the Specify Active Workset dialog box if it displays.

9. Zoom in on the elevator in the upper right of the building.

10. Move the core's north wall approximately **300mm** up.

11. In the Quick Access Toolbar, click ⊟ (Save) to save the local file.

12. **User1**, type **RL** (Reload Latest). There are no new changes to load because User2 has not saved back to the central model. In the No New Changes dialog box, click **Close**.

13. **User2** will click 🗗 (Synchronize Now). This saves the changes to the central model without relinquishing the User-Created Worksets (Core & Stair Walls workset).

Task 6: Request permission to edit.

1. **User1**, open the Worksets dialog box.

2. Select **Core & Stair Walls** in the list of worksets and click **Open**. Click **OK** to exit the dialog box.

3. Type **RL** (Reload Latest) again. This time, the core wall moves in response to the change made by **User2**.

4. Try to move the core wall back to its previous position. An error message opens that cannot be ignored. **User2** has made the Core & Stair Walls workset editable. Therefore, no one else can edit elements in it without permission, as shown in Figure 4–115.

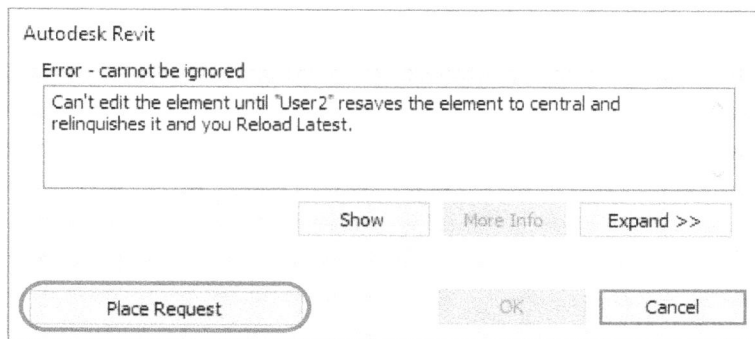

Figure 4–115

5. Click **Place Request**. The Editing Request Placed dialog box opens. Leave the dialog boxes opened, as shown in Figure 4–116.

Figure 4–116

6. **User2** now has a number **1** next to the **Editing Request** icon in the Status Bar, as shown in Figure 4–117. Click (Editing Request) to open the Editing Requests dialog box.

Figure 4–117

- Alternatively, an Editing Request Received alert should display that can be used to access the Editing Requests dialog box, but it may be off screen.

7. Expand the nodes to view more details about the request, as shown in Figure 4–118. Move the dialog box out of the way, if needed, to see the wall is highlighted.

Figure 4–118

8. Select the first node under **Others' pending Requests** and click **Grant** to give **User1** permission to modify the placement of this core wall. By doing so, you enable the other user to have full control over this one element in the workset.

9. **User1** will get an Editing Request Placed dialog box with a *Your request has been granted* message.

10. Close the Editing Request Placed dialog box. Because your request was granted, the core wall moves.

11. Move the core wall again. This time, you are not prompted to ask permission to move the core wall because you are still borrowing it.

12. Try to move another core wall. You do not have permission to move this wall. Click **Cancel** rather than place the request. The core wall returns to its original location.

Task 7: View information about the worksets.

1. **User1**, in the Status Bar, expand the Worksharing Display, and select **Owners**, as shown in Figure 4–119.

Figure 4–119

2. The view displays in color showing the two owners. Different colors highlight the elements and their respective owners, as shown in Figure 4–120. Hover the cursor over one of the walls to display information about the owner.

Figure 4–120

3. Open the Worksets dialog box. The owner of Core & Stair Walls is listed as **User2**, but **User1** is also listed as a borrower. Click **Cancel**.

4. Toggle the Worksharing Display off and zoom out to see the full building.

5. In the *Collaborate* tab>Manage Collaboration panel, click (Gray Inactive Worksets) to gray out the elements that you cannot modify without requesting permission. This also grays out the core walls, although you have a right to edit the wall that you borrowed.

6. Click (Synchronize and Modify Settings) and verify that all of the worksets will be relinquished before clicking **OK**.

7. Close the project.

8. **User2**, click (Synchronize Now). The core wall moves to the location selected by **User1**. When you sync with the central model, it also reloads the latest changes.

9. Close the project. When the Editable Elements dialog box opens, select **Relinquish elements and worksets**.

End of practice

Practice 4f
Work in a Workshared Project - MEP

Practice Objectives

- Work in pairs to simulate a worksharing environment.
- Update an existing central model for use in the practice.
- Create a local file of the central model from each copy of the software.

In this practice, you will need to work in pairs to simulate a worksharing environment. On your individual machines, User1 and User2 will each create a local file and select specific worksets to open in each project, as shown in Figure 4–121. One user within the pair will create the central model.

> **NOTE: Special Instructions for Instructors and Students**
> - Instructors: You will need to create a shared network folder for students to work in pairs to simulate the work environment.
> - Students: If this is self-paced training and you are not able to work in pairs or save a central model to a shared network location, you can watch the **Work in a Workshared Project-Architectural.mp4** video, located in the practice files *Videos* folder, for a demonstration of the tasks in the Architectural practice.

"User1" and "User2" are referenced throughout the practice but you will see your unique Revit username instead.

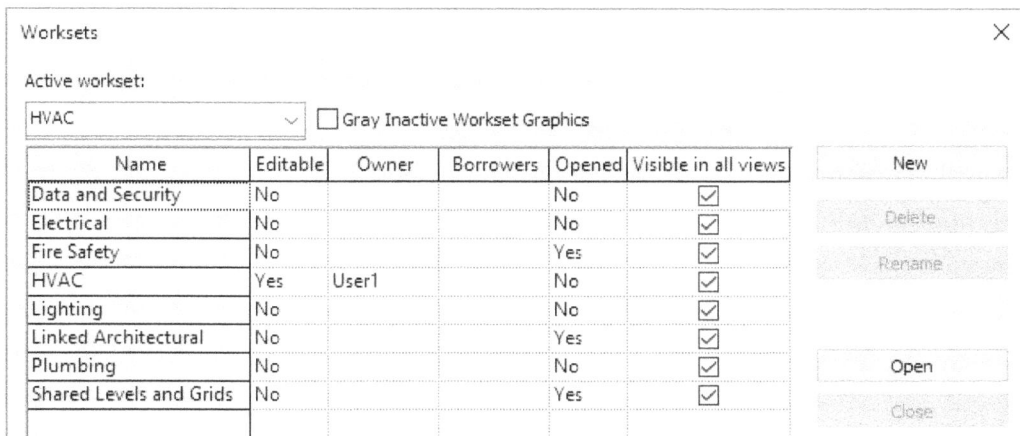

Name	Editable	Owner	Borrowers	Opened	Visible in all views
Data and Security	No			No	☑
Electrical	No			No	☑
Fire Safety	No			Yes	☑
HVAC	Yes	User1		No	☑
Lighting	No			No	☑
Linked Architectural	No			Yes	☑
Plumbing	No			No	☑
Shared Levels and Grids	No			Yes	☑

Worksets

Active workset: HVAC   ☐ Gray Inactive Workset Graphics

New / Delete / Rename / Open / Close

Figure 4–121

This practice uses a project that has been subdivided into worksets. To simulate a worksharing environment, work in groups of two. To keep the practices simple, the terms "User1" and "User2" will be used to indicate which user is to do certain tasks.

- **User1** updates the central model and focuses on the HVAC portion of the project.

- **User2** focuses on the lighting portion of the project.

Task 1: Open and save the central model to the shared folder location.

1. **User1**, verify that no projects are open. On the Home screen, in the *MODELS* section, click **Open...**. In the practice files *MEP* folder, open **Elementary-School-MEP-M.rvt**.

2. Alert boxes about a **Copied Central Model** and/or **Cannot Find Central Model** might display. Read and then close the alert boxes.

   - A central model needs to be repathed if it has been relocated. You will typically not have to do this in a work environment, but will need to do it for this practice to work.

3. In the *File* tab, expand 🖫 (Save As) and click 🖼 (Project).

4. In the Save As dialog box, click **Options...**.

5. In the File Save Options dialog box, select **Make this a Central Model after save** and then click **OK**.

6. Verify that the name is still set to **Elementary-School-MEP-M.rvt**, navigate to the shared network folder location, and click **Save**.

7. When the Workset File Already Exists dialog box displays, click **Yes** to replace the existing file.

8. Close the project.

Task 2: Create the local file for User1.

1. **User1** continues working within Revit.

2. In the Quick Access Toolbar, click 📂 (Open). Navigate to the shared network folder location and select **Elementary-School-MEP-M.rvt**.

3. Verify that **Create New Local** is selected and click **Open**.

4. In the *Collaborate* tab>Manage Collaboration panel or in the Status Bar, click 🗐 (Worksets).

5. In the Worksets dialog box, make **HVAC** the Active workset. Set *Editable* to **Yes** and select **Visible in all views** for this workset.

6. Select all the other worksets except **Linked Architectural** and **Shared Levels and Grids**. Click **Close** so that the worksets are not open in this session, as shown in Figure 4–122.

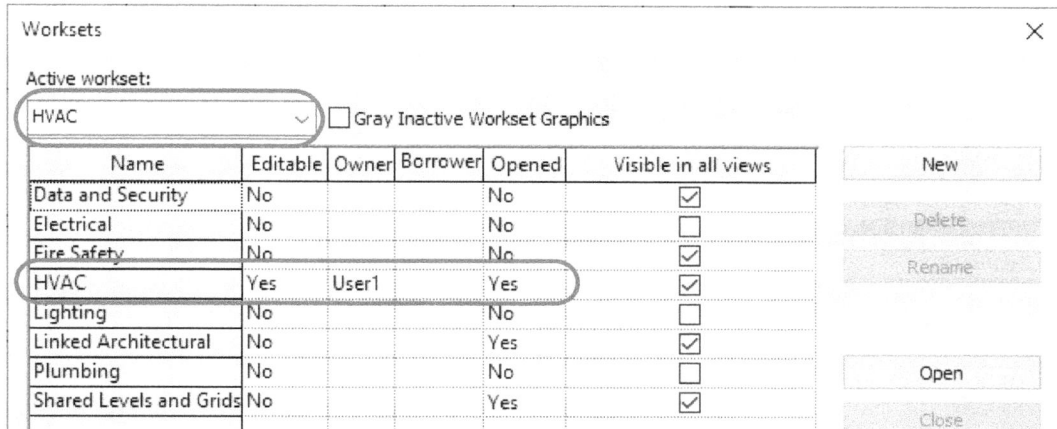

Worksets								

Active workset:

HVAC   ☐ Gray Inactive Workset Graphics

Name	Editable	Owner	Borrower	Opened	Visible in all views		New
Data and Security	No			No	☑		
Electrical	No			No	☐		Delete
Fire Safety	No			No	☑		
HVAC	Yes	User1		Yes	☑		Rename
Lighting	No			No	☐		
Linked Architectural	No			Yes	☑		
Plumbing	No			No	☐		Open
Shared Levels and Grids	No			Yes	☑		
							Close

Figure 4–122

7. Click **OK** to finish.

8. In the Quick Access Toolbar, click 💾 (Save) to save the local file.

9. Keep the file open.

Task 3: Create the local file for User2.

1. **User2**, in the Quick Access Toolbar, click 🗁 (Open). Navigate to the shared network folder location and select the file **Elementary-School-MEP-M.rvt**. Verify that **Create New Local** is selected.

2. Click the arrow next to **Open**, and select **Specify...** in the drop-down list, as shown in Figure 4–123.

Open	▼	Cancel

Workset:

    All

    Editable

✓   Last Viewed

    Specify...

Figure 4–123

3. Click **Open** to open the project.

4. In the Opening Worksets dialog box, select the **Data and Security**, **Fire Safety**, **HVAC**, and **Plumbing** worksets and click **Close** so that these worksets are not opened in this session, as shown in Figure 4–124.

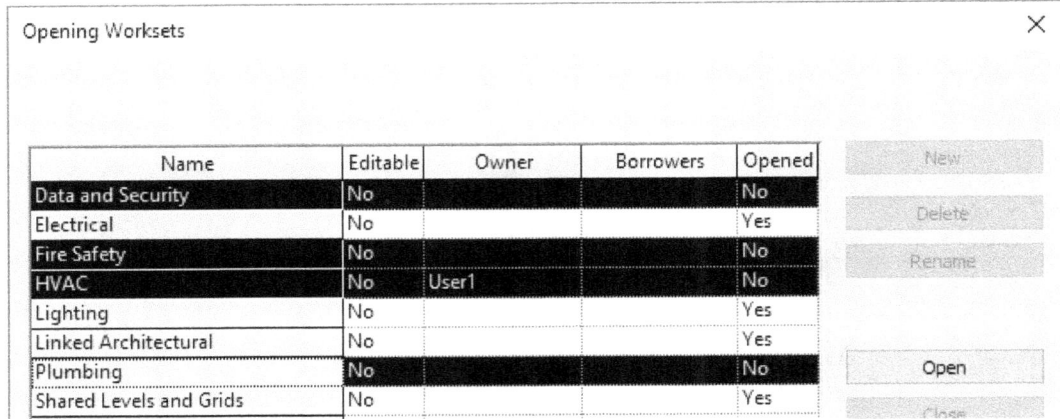

Name	Editable	Owner	Borrowers	Opened	
Data and Security	No			No	New
Electrical	No			Yes	Delete
Fire Safety	No			No	Rename
HVAC	No	User1		No	
Lighting	No			Yes	
Linked Architectural	No			Yes	
Plumbing	No			No	Open
Shared Levels and Grids	No			Yes	Close

Figure 4–124

5. Click **OK** to finish.

Note: The file name at the top of your Revit user interface should have your unique username at the end.

6. Save the local file and keep it opened.

Task 4: Add and modify elements in worksets.

1. **User1**, in your local file for **Elementary-School-MEP-M**, open the Coordination>MEP> **Ceiling Plans:01 RCP** view.

2. Zoom in on the lower left classroom. You should see elements related to HVAC. (If you do not, open the Worksets dialog box and ensure that the HVAC workset is opened.)

3. Move the second row of air terminals one ceiling grid to the left, similar to that shown in Figure 4–125. Reattach the flex duct, if required.

Figure 4–125

4. Open the Worksets dialog box and select the Lighting workset. Open it and verify it is visible in all views. Click **OK**. Now the air terminals are on top of the lights.

5. Move the lighting fixtures so they do not conflict with the air terminal.

6. Open the Worksets dialog box. **User1** is noted as the *Owner* of the **HVAC** workset and a *Borrower* of the **Lighting** workset, as shown in Figure 4–126.

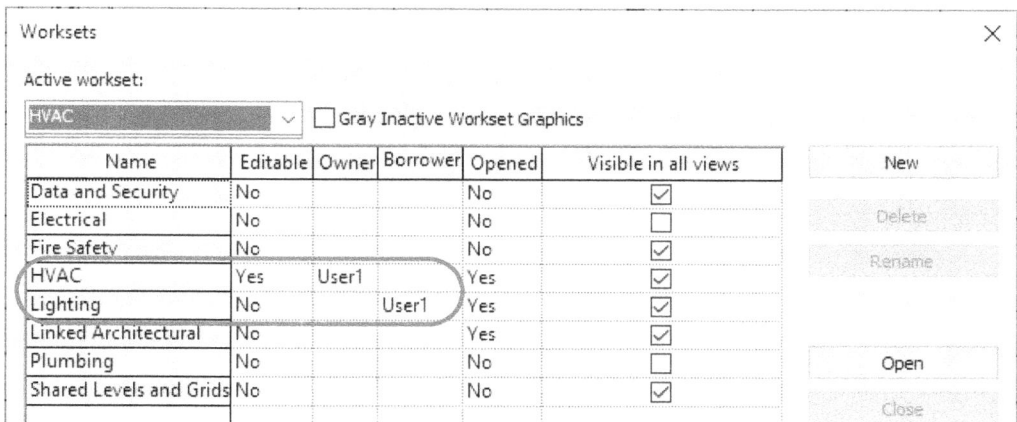

Figure 4–126

7. Click **OK** to close the dialog box.

8. In the *Collaborate* tab>Synchronize panel or the Quick Access Toolbar, click

    (Synchronize and Modify Settings) to open the Synchronize with Central dialog box, as shown in Figure 4–127. (Your central model location may differ from that in the figure.) The **Borrowed Elements** option should be selected and the **User-created Worksets** option should not be selected. Add a comment about moving the air terminals and light fixtures and select **Save Local File before and after synchronizing with central**. Click **OK**.

Synchronize with Central	✕
Central Model Location:	
Collaboration Tools Practice Files\Elementary-School-MEP-M.rvt	Browse...
☐ Compact Central Model (slow)	
After synchronizing, relinquish the following worksets and elements:	
☐ Project Standard Worksets ☐ View Worksets	
☐ Family Worksets ☐ User-created Worksets	
☑ Borrowed Elements	
Comment:	
Moved air terminals and light fixtures	
☑ Save Local File before and after synchronizing with central	
OK Cancel Help	

Figure 4–127

Task 5: Check out a workset.

1. **User2**, open the Coordination>MEP>**Ceiling Plans: 01 RCP** view in your local file. Zoom in to the lower-left classrooms. Neither the HVAC elements nor the changes show in the local file.

2. In the *Collaborate* tab>Synchronize panel, click (Reload Latest or type **RL**. The light fixture location changes but you do not see the air terminals because that workset is not open.

3. Click (Worksets) to open the dialog box and open the HVAC workset. Verify that it is **Visible in all views**.

4. Select **Lighting** in the *Active workset* drop-down list and make it editable (select **Yes** in the *Editable* column). The *Owner* should display as **User2**, as shown in Figure 4–128.

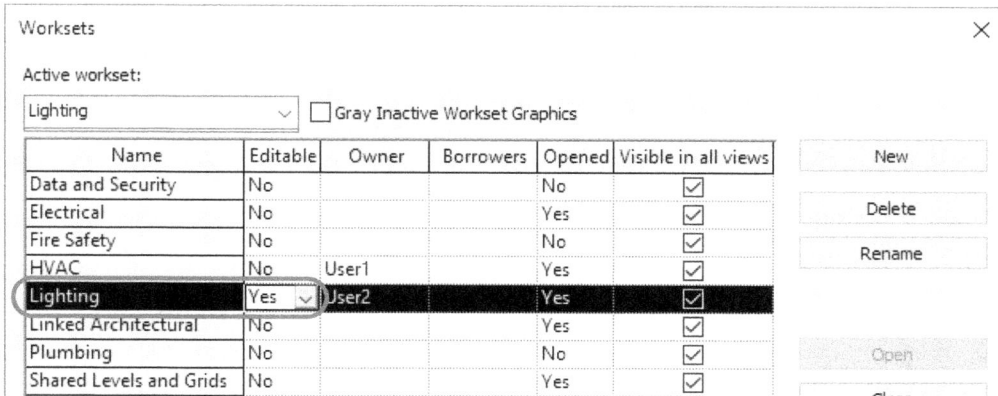

Figure 4–128

5. Click **OK** to close the dialog box.

6. Add another lighting fixture in the room.

7. In the Quick Access Toolbar, click 💾 (Save) to save the local file.

8. **User1**, type **RL** (Reload Latest). There are no new changes to load, as shown in Figure 4–129, because User2 has not saved back to the central model. Close the dialog box.

Figure 4–129

9. **User2** will click 📦 (Synchronize Now). This saves the changes to the central model without relinquishing the Lighting workset.

Task 6: Request permission to edit.

1. **User1**, type **RL** (Reload Latest) again. This time, the new lighting fixture displays because it was saved to the central model.

2. Try to move one of the lighting fixtures. This time, an error message displays that cannot be ignored, as shown in Figure 4–130. **User2** has made the Lighting workset editable. Therefore, no one else can edit elements in it without permission.

Figure 4–130

3. Click **Place Request**. The Editing Request Placed dialog box opens. Leave it open, as shown in Figure 4–131.

Figure 4–131

4. **User2** now gets a number **1** next to the **Editing Request** icon in the Status Bar, as shown in Figure 4–132. Click (Editing Request) to open the Editing Requests dialog box.

Figure 4–132

- Alternatively, an Editing Request Received alert should display that can be used to access the Editing Requests dialog box, but it may be off screen.

5. Expand the nodes to view more details about the request, as shown in Figure 4–133. Move the dialog box out of the way, if needed, to see the lighting fixture is highlighted.

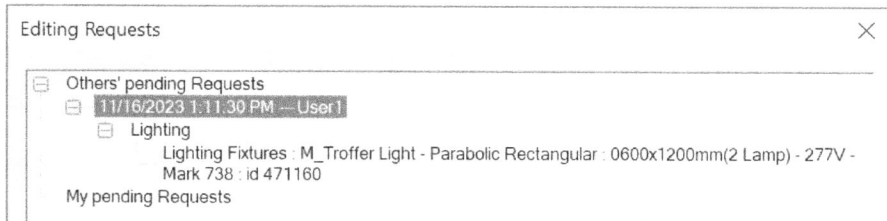

```
Editing Requests                                                              ×

    Others' pending Requests
        11/16/2023 1:11:30 PM — User1
            Lighting
                Lighting Fixtures : M_Troffer Light - Parabolic Rectangular : 0600x1200mm(2 Lamp) - 277V -
                Mark 738 : id 471160
    My pending Requests
```

Figure 4–133

6. Select the first node under **Others' pending Requests** and click **Grant** to give **User1** permission to modify the placement of this lighting fixture. By doing so, you enable the other user to have full control over this element in the workset.

7. **User1** will get an Editing Request Placed dialog box with a *Your request has been granted* message, as shown in Figure 4–134.

```
Editing Request Placed                          ×

        Your request has been granted.

Autodesk R

Error - cann

Can't edit
relinquish

                                                                    nd >>

            Pl              Close                      Cancel
```

Figure 4–134

8. Close the Editing Request Placed dialog box. Because your request was granted, the lighting fixture moves.

9. Move the lighting fixture again to exactly where you want it. This time, you are not prompted to ask to move the element because you are still borrowing it.

10. Try to move another lighting fixture. You do not have permission to move this or any others. Click **Cancel** rather than place the request. The lighting fixture returns to its original location.

Task 7: View information about the worksets.

1. In the View Control Bar, expand the Worksharing Display and click ⚐ (Owners). Different colors highlight the elements and their respective owners. Hover the cursor over one of the elements to display the information about the owner, as shown in Figure 4–135.

Figure 4–135

- The color on your display might be different.

2. Click 🔄 (Synchronize and Modify Settings) and relinquish **User-created Worksets** and **Borrowed Elements.**

3. Toggle the Worksharing Display off and zoom out to see the full building.

4. Save the local file.

5. **User2**, click 🔄 (Synchronize Now). The lighting fixture moves to the location where **User1** moved it. When you save to the central model, it also reloads the latest changes.

6. Close the project. When the Editable Elements dialog box opens, as shown in Figure 4–136, click **Relinquish elements and worksets**.

Figure 4–136

7. Close the project.

End of practice

4.9 Best Practices for Worksharing

Working with Company Policies

There are different practices regarding the frequency of synchronizing with the central model. Some companies ask users to synchronize before lunch and at the end of the day. Other companies require users to synchronize every 30 to 60 minutes. As the file size gets larger, synchronizing more often prevents the loss of data and also makes the synchronization finish quicker than if there are several hours worth of work to synchronize. However, there can be many reasons to change this frequency or to do additional synchronizations at specific points in time. They are:

- Major or critical changes to the project, such as moving an elevator core, reorienting the building on the site, etc.

- Users working in close proximity inside the model, to reduce permission issues.

When users need to leave their work for an hour or more (for lunch or a meeting or at the end of the day), it is best to synchronize and relinquish all. Then, upon returning, they should create a new local file (with a new name if you want the previous file saved as a backup). This ensures their file is up to date and eliminates the update time.

Tips for Using Worksets

Working with the Local File

- Be selective about which worksets you open. Avoid opening worksets that are not required for the work you are doing in the project. Limiting the number of worksets that will be opened with the file speeds up the process of opening and saving the file.

- Close unused views on a regular basis.

- Use a Starting View that is a drafting view, 2D plan, or elevation view. Revit only loads into memory what it displays, so this saves memory the next time the file is opened. This can also be used before plotting to increase the amount of available RAM.

- If you have been away from an active project for some time, it is better to create a new local file rather than depend on the **Reload Latest** command to update your current local file for you.

- If you are not sure what workset to put certain elements in, you can use *Workset1* or a specific temporary workset to put them in until the decision can be finalized.

- Restart the software before performing memory-intensive operations, such as printing an entire document set.

Saving to the Central Model

- Stagger syncing to the central model among users so that they are not saving concurrently.

- Type **RL** (Reload Latest) to update your copy of the project without changing the central model. This saves time by eliminating the need to reload as part of the **Synchronize and Modify Settings** command.

- Periodically synchronize with the central model using the **Compact File** option. This takes longer to save, but frees up more memory.

- If you get an error, such as *Unable to Save* or *File not found*, you might have run out of memory. Close the major worksets and view so that Revit releases some of the virtual memory that can be used to then save the file.

Requesting Edits

- Enable elements, not worksets, whenever possible. Revit automatically borrows the unowned elements without user intervention. This saves time by not having to request an edit in the first place.

- Communicate with the team members working on a project to avoid working on the same elements at the same time.

Tips for Creating Worksets

Worksets and the Team

- Assign one person to enable worksharing and create worksets and the central model.

- Create your project team structure to correspond with the new way of working with the building model. For example, architects and engineers do much of the work directly without needing an intern or drafter to create working drawings until the later parts of a project.

- Divide worksets according to components of a building rather than drawing types (such as plans, elevations, and sections), as these are created automatically.

- Key considerations when determining how to divide a project into worksets include the ability to load only those worksets that are required at the time and the ability to control visibility by worksets.

- As the project progresses, more worksets can be added.

- Using worksets does not negate the need for good team communication. You still need to have scheduling and planning meetings.

- Be sure that everyone knows which part of the model they are responsible for.

- File sharing should be a tool that is used in the workflow of the project; it should not be something that is disruptive.

Creating Worksets

- A multi-floor building does not need to have a workset for each floor until you are working on the floor-specific layouts.

- If you have a project with a large floor plate that needs to be divided by match lines to fit on sheets, you should divide the various parts of the building into separate worksets.

- If you have imported files into a project, each import should be in a separate workset that is not visible by default. They should also be closed when not in use.

- Every linked file should be in a separate workset not visible by default. They should also be closed when not in use.

- Worksets cannot be included in templates.

Default Workset Visibility

- As you create worksets, you should set the visibility. For example, the exterior and core of a building should be visible in all views, but furniture layouts or tenant partitions only need to be visible in specific views.

- Set up a standard for typical workset visibility designations. There are always exceptions, but working with the standard first is simpler.

Ending the Day

IMPORTANT: When you have finished working on the project for the day, you need to save, synchronize to central, and relinquish all borrowed and user-created worksets. If you are working on a project with other people, you need to relinquish all your worksets when closing a project so they can edit them if needed.

- When you close a project, if you did not relinquish elements and all worksets when you saved to the central model, the alert shown in Figure 4–137 will display.

Figure 4–137

- To relinquish worksets without saving to the central model, in the *Collaborate* tab> Synchronize panel, click ⬚ (Relinquish All Mine).

  Note: Do not delete any files in these directories.

- The backup directory for central models and local files, as shown in Figure 4–138, holds information about the editability of worksets, borrowed elements, and workset/element ownership. If required, you can restore the backup directory. In the *Collaboration* tab> Synchronize panel, click ⬚ (Restore Backup).

Folders	×	Name ▲
☐ 📁 Revit Class Files	⌃	📄 0_9741.rws
📁 Condo-Project_backup		📄 4_13.rws
📁 Condo Project_user1_backup		📄 7_6 rws
📁 Condo-Project_user2_backup		📄 8_0 rws
		📄 basicfileirfo.0018.dat
		📄 basicfileirfo.0019.dat
		📄 Condo-Project.slog
		📄 contents.0008.dat
		📄 contents.0009.dat
		📄 elemtable.0013.dat
		📄 elemtable.0019.dat

Figure 4–138

Chapter Review Questions

1. When setting up a project to be workshared, which of the following is performed first?

   a. Use Save As and, in Options, select **Make this a Central Model** after save.

   b. Start the project using a Central Model template.

   c. Use the Collaborate tool to enable worksharing, then use the **Worksets** command and add worksets.

   d. All of the grid lines and levels need to be in place.

2. Where should a central model be located?

   a. On your computer.

   b. On the company server.

   c. On each of the computers used by the team.

3. When you want to update the work that you have done and receive any changes others have made, but you do not want to change anything else, which command do you use?

   a. (Synchronize and Modify Settings)

   b. (Synchronize Now)

   c. (Relinquish All Mine)

   d. (Reload Latest)

4. Where should a local file be located?

   a. On the project manager's computer.

   b. On the company server.

   c. On each team member's computer.

5. What do you need to do so that any new elements you add are placed in a particular workset?

    a. Gray out inactive worksets so you know not to work in them.

    b. Make the workset editable.

    c. Set the workset as active.

    d. Create a new workset.

6. When selecting an element to edit, the icon shown in Figure 4–139 displays. What do you need to do?

Figure 4–139

    a. You can either edit the element without checking it out if it is not owned by someone else or place a request to edit it if it is owned by someone else.

    b. Click the icon and an error dialog box displays indicating that you cannot edit the element.

    c. Click the icon and an error dialog box displays indicating that you cannot edit the element, but you can request permission to edit it.

    d. Click the icon and a dialog box displays granting you permission to edit the element.

7. You have the most recent updates from the central model but some elements in a workset are not displaying, as shown in Figure 4–140. Which of the following should you do? (Select all that apply.)

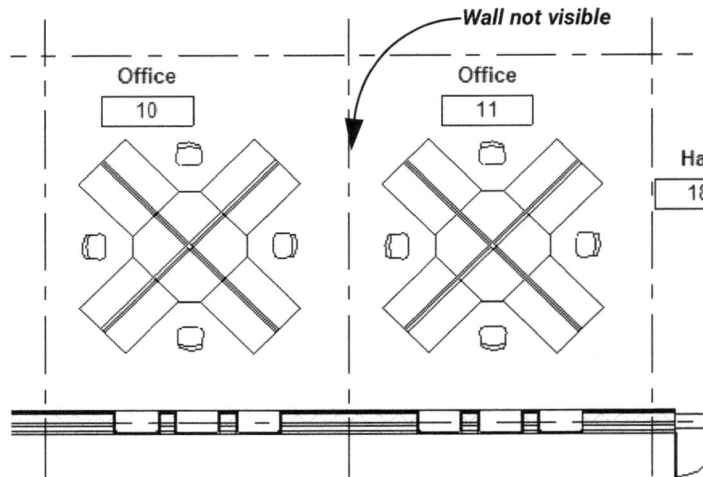

Figure 4–140

a. In the Visibility/Graphic Overrides dialog box, change the Visibility Setting of the workset to **Visible**.

b. In the Worksets dialog box, request permission to edit.

c. Set the workset as active.

d. In the Status Bar, change the Worksharing Display.

e. In the Worksets dialog box, verify if the workset is open.

Command Summary

Button	Command	Location
	Collaborate	• **Ribbon**: *Collaborate* tab>Manage Collaboration panel
	Editing Requests	• **Ribbon**: *Collaborate* tab>Synchronize panel • **Status Bar**
	Gray Inactive Worksets	• **Ribbon**: *Collaborate* tab>Manage Collaboration panel
	Owners (Display)	• **Status Bar:** expand Worksharing Display Off
	Relinquish All Mine	• **Ribbon**: *Collaborate* tab>Synchronize panel
	Reload Latest	• **Ribbon**: *Collaborate* tab>Synchronize panel • **Shortcut**: RL
	Restore Backup	• **Ribbon**: *Collaborate* tab>Synchronize panel
	Show History	• **Ribbon**: *Collaborate* tab>Synchronize panel
	Synchronize and Modify Settings	• **Quick Access Toolbar** • **Ribbon**: *Collaborate* tab>Synchronize panel, expand Synchronize with Central
	Synchronize Now	• **Quick Access Toolbar** • **Ribbon**: *Collaborate* tab>Synchronize panel, expand Synchronize with Central
	Worksets	• **Ribbon**: *Collaborate* tab>Manage Collaboration panel • **Status Bar**
	Worksets (Display)	• **Status Bar:** expand Worksharing Display Off
	Worksharing Display Off	• **Status Bar**

Index

www.ingramcontent.com/pod-product-compliance
Lightning Source LLC
Chambersburg PA
CBHW080926220326
41598CB00034B/5697

* 9 7 8 1 9 5 9 5 0 4 9 3 1 *